History teaches students how to write, how to analyze evidence, how to participate as a citizen, and why America is exceptional—for all the good and bad reasons. This book welcomes teachers and educators of all stripes into a vibrant online community, encourages them to embrace history, and shows them how to bring history to life in a fun and engaging way. So many teachers (and citizens!) believe in the power of history but aren't sure how to use it in the classroom. This book is the answer.

–Dr. Lindsay M. Chervinsky, presidential historian
and author of *The Cabinet: George Washington and
the Creation of an American Institution*

This book was a joy to read. You can feel the authors' love of history and passion for student learning jumping off each page. Stories from the classroom (especially the civics example) remind us how important and impactful an engaged and enthusiastic history teacher can be for young people. Many of the lessons—about historical empathy, building community, practicing informed civic engagement—transcend age and grade level. I can't wait to bring some of these principles into my college classroom!

–Jane Hong, Associate Professor of History, Occidental College

Karalee and Laurel pack the pages of this book full of practical strategies, tools to empower, and activities that create community, foster connections, plus build awareness and empathy! *Bring History and Civics to Life* is an incredible book that will help you move from "why" to "how" and see new possibilities to explore history and honor the stories and people that came before—all while teaching best practices to structure and frame conversations, showing you how to guide classroom activities to create safe spaces, and establishing community practices to help facilitate meaningful learning experiences. This is a must-read for every educator on a journey to help students become informed and empathetic citizens.

–Ann Kozma, @annkozma723, Educator Innovation Lead, Flip | Microsoft"

I'm not a techie—which is why I'm so thrilled to see this masterful guide to using tech to enhance civic learning. It's hard to believe that Karalee Wong Nakatsuka was ever a beginner herself, which should give every educator more confidence. As a constitutional scholar, I'm grateful to the authors for helping educators make our nation's history and charters more accessible to all. We need digitally and civically empowered Americans now more than ever!

–Linda R. Monk, J.D., author of *The Bill of Rights: A User's Guide*

*Bring History and Civics to Life* is an essential tool for pre-service and in-service teachers, and methods professors. The resources provided in this book demonstrate how teachers can use technology in a civically responsible manner that fosters historical inquiry and community. The ISTE standards are critical to the education courses I teach, especially with the proliferation of online teaching and learning since the COVID-19 pandemic. Karalee Wong Nakatsuka and Laurel Aguilar-Kirchhoff masterfully unpack these standards with reflection, compassion, and encouragement in order to demonstrate how implementing technology can promote critical thinking, historical empathy, civic engagement, and active citizenship.

–Katherine Perrotta, Ph.D., Assistant Professor of Middle Grades and Secondary Education (Social Studies), Mercer University Tift College of Education

Jam-packed with big ideas and powerful strategies! Using this book as a roadmap doesn't just prepare our learners for future "real world" experiences, it empowers learners to connect to the world now as historians, community builders, and civically engaged leaders. If you are ready to cultivate a community of inquiry focused on nurturing the whole child and developing a historical empathy mindset, this is the book for you. Highly recommend!

–Lainie Rowell, educator, author, and international consultant

# BRING HISTORY & CIVICS TO LIFE

## Lessons & Strategies to Cultivate Informed, Empathetic Citizens

### Karalee Wong Nakatsuka and Laurel Aguilar-Kirchhoff

**International Society for Technology in Education**

PORTLAND, OREGON • ARLINGTON, VIRGINIA

Book Title: *Bring History and Civics to Life*
Subtitle: Lessons and Strategies to Cultivate Informed, Empathetic Citizens
Author Names: Karalee Wong Nakatsuka and Laurel Aguilar-Kirchhoff
© 2022 International Society for Technology in Education

Acquisitions Editor: Valerie Witte
Editor: Stephanie Argy
Copy Editor: Lisa Hein
Proofreader: Joanna Szabo
Indexer: Kento Ikeda
Book Design and Production: Olivia M. Hammerman
Cover Design: Beth DeWilde
Peer Reviewers: Valencia Abbott, James Allen, CherylAnne Amendola, Shannon Salter Burghardt, Lisa C. Camichos, Mickey Chavannes, Matt Di Giulio, John Padula

Library of Congress Cataloging-in-Publication Data

Library of Congress Cataloging-in-Publication Data

Names: Nakatsuka, Karalee Wong, author. | Aguilar-Kirchhoff, Laurel, author.
Title: Bring history and civics to life : lessons and strategies to cultivate informed, empathetic citizens / Karalee Wong Nakatsuka and Laurel Aguilar-Kirchhoff.
Identifiers: LCCN 2022021479 (print) | LCCN 2022021480 (ebook) | ISBN 9781564849359 (trade paperback) | ISBN 9781564849441 (epub) | ISBN 9781564849458 (pdf)
Subjects: LCSH: History--Study and teaching (Elementary)--United States. | History--Study and teaching (Secondary)--United States. | Civics--Study and teaching (Elementary)--United States. | Civics--Study and teaching (Secondary)--United States. | Educational technology.
Classification: LCC LB1582.U6 N36 2022 (print) | LCC LB1582.U6 (ebook) | DDC 372.890973--dc23/eng/20220803
LC record available at https://lccn.loc.gov/2022021479
LC ebook record available at https://lccn.loc.gov/2022021480

First Edition
ISBN: 978-1-56484-935-9
Ebook version available

Printed in the United States of America

ISTE® is a registered trademark of the International Society for Technology in Education.

# CONTENTS

# ABOUT ISTE

The International Society for Technology in Education (ISTE) is home to a passionate community of global educators who believe in the power of technology to transform teaching and learning, accelerate innovation and solve tough problems in education.

ISTE inspires the creation of solutions and connections that improve opportunities for all learners by delivering: practical guidance, evidence-based professional learning, virtual networks, thought-provoking events and the ISTE Standards. ISTE is also the leading publisher of books focused on technology in education. For more information or to become an ISTE member, visit iste.org. Subscribe to ISTE's YouTube channel and connect with ISTE on Twitter, Facebook and LinkedIn.

**RELATED ISTE TITLES**

*Developing Digital Detectives: Essential Lessons for Discerning Fact From Fiction in the 'Fake News' Era,* by Jennifer LaGarde and Darren Hudgins (2021)

*Teach Boldly: Using Edtech for Social Good,* by Jennifer Williams (2019)

*Digital Citizenship in Action: Empowering Students to Engage in Online Communities,* by Kristen Mattson (2017)

To see all books available from ISTE, please visit iste.org/books.

# ABOUT THE AUTHORS

**Laurel Aguilar-Kirchhoff, MS.Ed.,** spent 20 years teaching history and science and now serves as a digital learning specialist, educational consultant, and adjunct university professor. Laurel works with educators, administrators, and students to successfully integrate educational technology into curriculum for lasting student learning outcomes. Her areas of expertise include digital citizenship, media literacy, blended learning, and curriculum instruction and design, as well as educational technology and innovation in the classroom. She was recognized as the 2018 National History Day—California Teacher of the Year, was a top six finalist for the National History Day Teacher of the Year, and was the Inland Area CUE Administrator of the Year in 2022. Laurel is a Google Certified Trainer, Leading Edge Certified Online Blended Teacher, and a member of the iCivics Education Network. Laurel previously served on the ISTE Digital Citizenship PLN Leadership team and continues as an ISTE Community Leader. Laurel seeks to educate, inspire, and empower education professionals to create a culture of learning, no matter the learning environment. When she's not teaching or training, Laurel enjoys spending time with her family and friends, attending and presenting at edtech and history conferences, and voraciously reading.

**Karalee Wong Nakatsuka, MA.Ed.,** has taught middle school U.S. History students since 1990. She is passionate about using technology to engage students, focusing on building community in her classroom, and helping students to see themselves in the story of America as they develop into empathetic and informed critical thinkers and citizens who make a difference in the world. In 2019, Karalee was recognized as the Gilder Lehrman History Teacher of the Year for California and was a top ten finalist for the national award. She serves on the America250 History Education Advisory Council, the Gilder Lehrman Teacher Advisory Council, the Monticello Teacher Advisory Group, and is a member of the iCivics Education Network. She is a ThingLink Certified Educator, amongst other edtech certifications.

Karalee was featured in *Time* magazine's September 2021 issue in the article "From Teachers to Custodians, Meet the Educators Who Saved a Pandemic School Year." When she's not teaching, she can be found enjoying history-related vacations with her family, collaborating with fellow history teachers locally and across the country, attending and presenting at conferences, and hanging out on Twitter.

# ACKNOWLEDGMENTS

We are thankful to so many who have been on this journey with us. If we were to mention them all by name, we would be writing another book. With hearts full of gratitude, here is our incomplete list of thank-yous.

Our ISTE team, including editors Stephanie Argy and Valerie Witte. Who knew developing, writing, and editing a book could be so much fun? Val, our poetic acquisitions editor, thank you for taking a chance on us and putting up with our countless Bitmojis. Steph, we can't think of a better person to sit on a Grecian beach with, snacking on Crunch Berries, and discussing the Oxford comma. You are one in a million and we are so fortunate to have you as our editor and friend.

Our amazing PLN, including our fantastic book contributors iCivics EdNet, #ssChat and #ssChatReads, #HistoryFoodies, #TwitterStorians, and #Edtech friends. We love collaborating, learning, and hanging out with all of you on Twitter and hopefully in "real life" very soon!

**Laurel:**

Karalee—thank you for your friendship and support, and for being an amazing coauthor. You took a chance on me, both as a friend and coauthor. We have had a wild ride bringing this book to life, and I truly wouldn't have wanted to go down this road with anyone else. We wrote a book!

To my wonderful husband and boys—you have supported me every step of the way while writing this book. The three of you have all of my heart.

Thank you to all my colleagues and friends who have taught me, helped me, ran copies for me, and supported me on all of my journeys. I am fortunate to have had so many wonderful colleagues over the years. There are too many to name individually here; I hope that you know how much you mean to me. I appreciate you more than I could ever write. To all my science and history colleagues and friends—you are amazing, and I appreciate you! My digital learning colleagues—thank you for your innovation and creativity. You constantly inspire me!

I would not have started on my National History Day journey without the help and guidance of my wonderful assistant principal, Mr. John Farr. My National History Day—California Leadership Team inspires and challenges me to innovate and create for all our students in California. Thank you Whitney, Craig, Christy, and many others for your leadership and friendship.

ISTE DigCit and Community Leaders—I have met the most amazing people through both serving as a ISTE DigCit PLN Incoming incoming copresident and through our journey to be a part of the ISTE Community Leadership Program. A special debt of gratitude and friendship to Jackie, Casey, and LeeAnn. Your friendship holds a special place in my heart.

To my students, past and present—thank you for allowing me to be your teacher. I have learned so much from you as well! I am honored to have played a small part in your educational journey.

**Karalee:**

I am so blessed by so many who supported and inspired me, helped me to find my history voice, and gave me the confidence to write this book. If we weren't limited to 40,000 words, I would thank each of you by name. My deepest gratitude to you all.

Lucy—your friendship is truly a pandemic blessing/silver lining. We both had no idea what it meant when I asked you to be my coauthor. I'm grateful that we could learn, grow, and have lots of fun on this journey as writers, collaborators, educators, citizens, moms, wives, and (most importantly) as friends; I'm excited for this next leg of our journey together. We wrote a book!

My dear family: Jimmy, Christopher, and Kristi—I couldn't have done this without your love, patience, prayers, and support. Love you all—I am truly blessed.

Dr. Jane Hong and Dr. Emma Humphries—amazing scholars, passionate citizens, and dear friends (always just a text or DM away) who have been instrumental in helping me to deepen my knowledge and understanding, build my self-confidence, and say yes.

Dr. Joanne Freeman—thank you for speaking up as a brilliant, friendly, and empathetic flesh-and-blood female role model for girls of all ages to follow; you inspire and motivate me to use my voice. And to the amazing NCHE History Matters community—thank you for the opportunity to deepen my history knowledge and have fun engaging in democracy together every Friday morning. History Matters. Community Matters. Yay History!

My Gilder Lehrman history teacher buddies—you are the perfect combination of inspiration, collaboration, support, and fun. We truly are #BetterTogether.

My wonderfully supportive extended family, friends, and colleagues past and present—thank you for the constant encouragement, checking in, support, and understanding. So grateful for you all.

To my frogtastic students, past, present, and future—you are the reason I wrote this book. You inspire me, you motivate me, you teach me, you make me laugh, and you cheer me on. Thank you for letting me share our classroom and your voices with the world.

*For all the history social science teachers out there.*

# FOREWORD

When it comes to understanding our world and our place in it, there is perhaps no greater or more productive pursuit than the study of history and civics. History allows us to make sense of the past, thereby helping us to better understand our present, while civics helps us understand our roles and duties as part of a self-governing society.

Simply put, history and civics are the study of life.

Yet of all of the subjects we teach in schools, few have been more in need of a little more life injected into them than history and civics. History and civics may be the study of life, but we oftentimes struggle to find a pulse when entering a history or civics class.

Luckily for all of us, Karalee Wong Nakatsuka and Laurel Aguilar-Kirchoff are willing to share their secrets to classroom resuscitation. In *Bring History and Civics to Life: Lessons and Strategies to Cultivate Informed, Empathetic Citizens*, they help us see that in order to bring history and civics to life, we must connect it to students' lives—we must allow students to see themselves in the narratives that constitute our history and in the systems and processes that form our government.

As they write, "We are passionate about demarginalizing history so that our students will see themselves, as well as others, in the diverse, inclusive, full story of history. In turn, it is our sincere wish that this will empower, inspire, and motivate [our students] to become actively engaged citizens who contribute to all of their communities."

I share the authors' passion. I currently serve as the Chief Education Officer for iCivics, an education nonprofit reimagining civic learning for American democracy. At iCivics, we believe each and every student can benefit from a civic education that both reflects and honors their identities and experiences, and helps in understanding and appreciating others' perspectives. We know that by helping students build connections to their own lives and experiences, we make civic education matter, and we provide tangible skills for success throughout students' lives and careers.

In providing "user-friendly and accessible" wisdom, Nakatsuka and Aguilar-Kirchoff provide just such connections to put knowledge into practice. Of course, "user-friendly and accessible" is just another way of saying "conversational and a pleasure to read," and that is precisely how I would describe *Bring History and Civics to Life*. It's a little book with a big heart that is a treasure trove of inspiration for social studies education nerds, both veteran and aspiring.

Reading this book feels like hanging out in the teachers' lounge on the Friday before Labor Day. Sure, there's a lot of excitement for the three-day weekend, but there's also that electric energy and hope that always precedes a new school year. Grab a fresh cup of coffee and join your colleagues in this exciting space. You'll immediately find that you have a friend and colleague in Nakatsuka and Aguilar-Kirchoff, and you'll be so glad you came.

# INTRODUCTION

# Setting the Stage

*Karalee Wong Nakatsuka*

*Laurel Aguilar-Kirchhoff*

Welcome! We're so happy you're here. We had a lot of fun writing this book together during a worldwide pandemic (mainly via Zoom and Google Meet), and we're excited you've decided to join our conversation. Grab your beverage of choice, be it coffee or Diet Coke like Laurel, or green tea or Cherry Coke like Karalee. Pull up a chair and make yourself comfortable. Since you've joined us and picked up our book, we now consider you a friend. You're part of our community, our Professional Learning Network (PLN). So let's get to know each other—we probably have a lot in common.

We, Laurel Aguilar-Kirchhoff and Karalee Wong Nakatsuka, have more than 50 combined years of experience in education, and we both have a lot to say. (Laurel is chuckling now—this is an understatement.) We are both experienced middle school history teachers and history moms, and we love talking history; if you hang out with us long enough, you will inevitably hear us debating about Thomas Jefferson or George Washington. (Now Karalee is chuckling at that one.) We spend a lot of time researching, discussing, and reflecting on edtech, accessibility, community, and civics, then applying our findings and best practices to all our spaces. When we're not in a pandemic, we enjoy presenting, learning, and interacting with our fellow tech and history friends at conferences and other in-person events. In fact, we first met at a history conference: the California Council for the Social Studies (CCSS). (It's a great story—we'll tell you all about it later in the book.) We can also be found hanging out on Twitter with our history and edtech friends (PLN). Come join us; it is chock-full of social studies teacher fun.

Join a PLN (Professional or Personalized Learning Network): a community that uses social media and technology to collect, communicate, collaborate, create, and connect colleagues (edut.to/3NGtiko)

Join your local and/or national social studies council. Take advantage of their professional development and attend their conferences. This is a great way to learn and improve your teaching practices, as well as to meet and interact with awesome history educators. (If you don't have a local or national social studies council, you can always find fellow history teachers through ISTE communities.) Karalee likes to say that history conferences are like History Teacher Disneyland—the happiest history place on earth!

History-Social Science Twitter has a wonderful online community. History-social science teachers and historians (#TwitterStorians) routinely share and interact with one another. It's a great opportunity to get new ideas, reflect on best practices, ask questions, and learn from each other. Resources and research are shared freely, and there are discussions on a variety of topics. You can start by following Laurel @LucyKirchh and Karalee @HistoryFrog on Twitter! Also, follow the hashtag #ssChat (an open conversation among Twitter social studies educators and a weekly Twitter chat) and see what your fellow history teachers are thinking.

The Gilder Lehrman Institute of American History (bit.ly/GilderLehrman) is a nonprofit organization dedicated to K-12 history education. Sign up for free to become an affiliate school and learn about and participate in their many free offers, resources, trainings, webinars, seminars, and more. Gilder Lehrman also hosts an annual National History Teacher of the Year Award (bit.ly/GilderNHTOY). Nominate a deserving colleague.

Take a moment to look at *Time* magazine's September 2021 article "From Teachers to Custodians, Meet the Educators Who Saved A Pandemic School Year" (bit.ly/TimeTeachers) and read the inspiring stories of K-12 educators and staff who went above and beyond to care for their students; you might even see a familiar face featured in one of the stories. Reflect on the lessons we all learned and can continue to apply in our classrooms.

## Why History, Civics, and Empathy are Important to Teach (Now More than Ever)

When we first envisioned this book, we imagined it would be about bringing history to life with technology. But we live in a historic moment of our own, and as we worked on the book in 2020 and 2021, the United States was embroiled in an election and political cycle like no other, as well as dealing with the ramifications (both educational and social-emotional) of a worldwide health crisis. As we researched and wrote, reflected and discussed (on the web and in video calls—hooray for technology!), we realized that the core of our book needed to shift so that we could also address history's role in promoting civics and citizenship through educational technology. Throughout history, it's been easy for people to other and dehumanize those who are not like them; we history and civics teachers have the opportunity to change this script and be more inclusive in our approach. We are passionate about demarginalizing history so that our students will see themselves, as well as others, in the diverse, inclusive, full story of history. In turn, it is our sincere wish that this will empower, inspire, and motivate them to become actively engaged citizens who contribute to all of their communities.

History education, civics education, and educational technology in the classroom are not new concepts. But is there a way for all three to come together to help our students become informed global citizens who participate in civics in a meaningful way? In an *EdTechReview* article, author Ananya Debroy writes, "Due to technology advancement, teachers have . . . options to use digital tools and projects that can connect students to the world in ways that promote a mind-set of taking action and applied learning" (Debroy, 2019). That is where *Bring History and Civics to Life* comes in. This book is designed to help educators from all over the world gain insight into historical empathy, community building, and civics, both in and out of the classroom, and to show how educational technology can bring these concepts to life for students. The ultimate goal is to provide opportunities for students to apply that learning in ways that promote civics and citizenship on a local, national, and global level.

## Who Is this Book For?

This book was written for all educators who are passionate about their teaching practices. We want to meet you where you are on your journey. This book is written for all levels of tech savvy—from the beginner to the most advanced. We have designed this book to be user-friendly and accessible. (We'd like to think of ourselves as user-friendly and accessible too!) Our mantra when writing this book was, "Start from where you are and go from there. . . . there is no such thing as perfection in edtech" (Nakatsuka, 2021).

While we, Karalee and Laurel, are both experienced U.S. History teachers, our goal for this book is to be accessible and user-friendly for all content areas in the social sciences and beyond. We encourage you to look at this book through the lens of your content area and make connections that seem relevant and meaningful to your current teaching assignment. Being a professional educator is a lifelong commitment to learning—both for ourselves as educators and for our students, especially as we find new ways to provide them with accessible, equitable, and meaningful learning. (We're sending you virtual high fives—we're passionate about teaching too, in case you haven't noticed by now.)

· · · · · · · · · · · · · · · · · · · · · · · · · · · · · · · · · · · ·

# Book Club!
## AN EXPERIENCE FROM KARALEE AND LAUREL

June 2020

The conversation was lively. The participants were engaged. It was early Saturday morning, and we enthusiastically participated in our history book club. The hour flew by; as we departed, we said our goodbyes and thanked the hosts and our friends for another thoughtful conversation. No, we weren't in the back room at the local library; we were on social media participating in a #ssChatReads online book club hosted via Twitter. We joined our virtual community of history-social science teachers from many geographic areas, as we sat in our own living rooms, connected to Wi-Fi, chatting through our laptops, all during a pandemic. Technology brought us together in a way that might never have happened in real life (IRL).

One book in particular made a huge impact on us both. For four weeks during the months of June and July 2020, we both woke up bright and early to join our #ssChatReads Twitter book club friends to discuss Erika Lee's *America for Americans: A History of Xenophobia in the United States*. The book was intense and thought-provoking. And though the topic was heavy, we both enjoyed and actively participated in the Twitter conversation. As we spent time with colleagues, we reflected on how our understanding of the past informs our present realities, our personal identities, and our actions as informed citizens. Technology provided the opportunity for us to connect, build community, and reflect on history's role in our lives. This type of access to technology will continue to allow us to shape our own approaches to historical perspectives and teaching practices, as well as to continue learning throughout our lives.

**IRL** (in real life) is an abbreviation to distinguish an interaction that happens in in-person reality, as opposed to a virtual interaction such as online on Twitter and other social platforms or a video chat/meeting through Zoom.

 #ssChatReads is an online Twitter book club, held on designated Saturday mornings at 7 a.m. PT | 10 a.m. ET. Participants are invited to follow the schedule, read the book that was selected, and then discuss the book together in a Q&A format via a virtual Twitter chat. You can check out the archive of #ssChatReads discussions here: bit.ly/ssChatReadsArchives. An informative article by Dr. Lindsay M. Chervinsky, historian, podcaster, speaker, and author of *The Cabinet*, explains "Why You Should Participate in an (Online) Book Club" (bit.ly/WhyBookClub).

## What's in This Book

This book is meant to provide thought-provoking ideas and resources, as well as relevant places to start or continue in your educational practice. We have divided it into two sections:

+ **Part 1: The "Why."** In chapters 1, 2, and 3 we explore the pedagogical and edtech connections to teaching and learning history-social science. You will find plenty of opportunities to reflect on your current educational practices so that you can foster historical inquiry, build community, and help your students connect to civic action.

- **Chapter 1: History**—Why is it important to teach history, and whose history are we teaching? How can educators help their students develop historical empathy?
- **Chapter 2: Community**—What does it mean to "build community"? How can educators create safe, welcoming, and supportive classroom environments? What are some community-building activities and resources?
- **Chapter 3: Civics**—How do we define "citizenship" and "civic education"? How can educators in all content areas incorporate a "civic mindset" into their subject areas? How does digital citizenship fit into all of this?

- **Part 2: The "How."** In chapters 4 and 5 we provide the opportunity for you to apply all you've learned after exploring and processing the "why" in the first few chapters. We will share an abundance of edtech tools with you and the space for you to apply your new insights and understandings as you work toward designing your own lesson.

  - **Chapter 4: Using Edtech for History, Civics, and Community Building**—This is a deeper dive into the world of edtech and history, but fear not! There is something for everyone at every level of edtech expertise.
  - **Chapter 5: Lesson Design and Inspiration**—Here is your opportunity to apply everything you've learned from chapters 1 through 4. We've provided a lesson template along with a sample lesson from both of us to help guide and inspire you as you design your own lesson to bring history and civics to life with edtech. This chapter also contains lesson plan ideas from outstanding, experienced educators from our PLN. We hope these will inspire you and provide ideas for you to apply in your own classroom.
  - **Conclusion: You Can Do This!**—Join our community! Spoiler alert: we tell our story of how we met, how we learned to

incorporate edtech into our own classes, and how you can do the same. (Karalee says it's a good story, you don't want to miss it.)

Each chapter has ideas and suggestions on how to incorporate edtech to help history and civics come to life for your students. You don't have to be an edtech expert to start this journey! You will see sidebars with in-depth information, definitions, and activities that correlate with the research, stories, and practices being discussed. At the end of each chapter, there is a #TryOneNewThingChallenge chart to help promote self-reflection and encourage you to try one new thing at the level that you feel most comfortable with right now. These easy-to-implement ideas will help you make changes for lasting educational impact in your classroom and approaches to teaching.

## HOW TO NAVIGATE THIS BOOK

We encourage you to read and use this book in a way that makes the most sense for you. You can read this book in any order that you wish. If you are new to teaching (or new to teaching in the history-social sciences), we recommend that you read this book in order, from cover to cover; the ideas and concepts build a cohesive picture of how to bring history and civics to life for your students. If you are a veteran teacher with more experience teaching history-social science, you can choose the educational adventure that will be most meaningful for you. You may want to skim the chapters and then return to a particular section that stands out to you. Laurel would start by flipping through the chapters to see all of the bulleted lists, charts, and tables of resources to share. Karalee would head straight to the stories and sidebars, hoping for a laugh and something to apply to her classroom right away. However you decide to read this book, we encourage you to utilize the resources and connections that are provided.

You will see QR codes (quick response codes) and Bitly links sprinkled throughout this book. These provide direct access to the materials and links we share. Some of the QR codes will also connect you to our wonderful companion website BringHistoryToLife.com, where we provide additional resources, expanded information, and so much more.

QR codes are scannable images that can be instantly read with a QR code scanner app or with most smartphone cameras. They can link to online content such as websites and applications. QR codes can be generated for free and are a great way to share content with students (bit.ly/GenerateQRCode).

Bitly is a URL (web address or link) shortener; people can shorten and customize longer links allowing for greater accessibility and the ability to share content more easily. Remember, Bitly links are case sensitive (bitly.com).

We also encourage you to take notes, grab resources, and reflect in a way that will be useful and meaningful for you as you read. Laurel would grab a few packs of her favorite sticky notes (in neon colors, of course) and fill them up with all the ideas and resources that resonate with her to create a visual map of the material to serve as placeholders in the book for her to return to and share with her students. (Karalee is smiling and nodding her head; you should see Laurel's books filled with a collection of colorful sticky notes!) Karalee would create a Wakelet (a digital folder; see the tip in the sidebar), take notes, and grab links to websites and resources that excite her, then promptly share them with her history buddies (sharing is caring). Grab a yellow legal pad, open a Google or Word document, or turn to the next blank sheet in your composition notebook and begin sketchnoting (see tip in the sidebar)—choose what works for you, and let us begin our adventure together.

As you grab resources via the numerous links sprinkled throughout our book, please be aware that bit.lys are case sensitive and must be typed exactly as they appear. You can also grab these wonderful resources with the QR codes provided.

Sketchnoting is a form of note-taking using doodles and text. Sylvia Duckworth offers an abundance of sketchnoting resources and tutorials on her website (bit.ly/SketchNoteClass). You can also check out Nichole Carter's book, *Sketchnoting in the Classroom: A Practical Guide to Deepen Student Learning*, published by ISTE.

Wakelet is a digital curation platform that allows users to collect, curate, and organize digital resources and moreeasily and efficiently. Wakelets can also be used collaboratively for content sharing. Think of it as a shared digital folder—collaborators can access the Wakelet and add content that is accessible to all collaborators. Classrooms on Wakelet allow teachers and students to share resources in a safe way (wakelet.com).

## ISTE Standards and Resources

The word "standards" puts some teachers on high alert for a multitude of reasons. In education, you can't get away from the word, which is used in so many ways and so many different contexts. Standards can refer to the quality of teaching, as well as to a concrete list of content area material that must be taught during a school term. While there are definite pros and cons to having defined learning standards for students, the term itself means a level of quality or attainment (Lexico).

In this book we will be utilizing the ISTE Standards for both Students and Educators as our pedagogical basis of understanding and a means to stream-line the conversations and resources. This is not to say that other standards or frameworks don't bring meaning to our work in the history-social science classroom. We also acknowledge that there are valuable resources and guidelines that are provided through the College, Career,  and Civic Life Framework (C3) (bit.ly/CThreeFramework), in addition to your own state/local content area standards. (Karalee says it's like CYOA: Choose your own standards/framework adventure! Some standards and frameworks are required—for example, content area standards. Other standards and frameworks may not be required but can help add meaning and guidance to improve our educational practices.)

"But what are the ISTE Standards?" you may be asking yourself. Laurel likes to envision the ISTE Standards as a set of guidelines for solid educational practices that are rooted in research and provide a roadmap for learning, teaching, and coaching with the use of technology. The ISTE Standards were written to "ensure that using technology for learning can create high-impact, sustainable, scalable and equitable learning experiences for all learners" iste.org/iste-standards). They are not a static set of standards; they are reviewed regularly for relevance. You may see updates and iterations of the ISTE Standards over time, but as of the writing of this book they have recently been updated to their most current format.

As you travel down the road of your own educational practices and learning, think of the ISTE Standards as a map, or as signs posted along the side of the roadway of education that help guide you in your practices and provide direction for your teaching and learning. Karalee finds this a comforting and inviting description: she pictures Laurel standing by the side of the road, holding up a sign with the ISTE Standards while she, seated in her car, glances back and forth along the Standards road, using these Standards road signs and her ISTE Standards GPS to successfully navigate along the educational highway.

The ISTE Standards were written to "ensure that using technology for learning can create high-impact, sustainable, scalable and equitable learning experiences for all learners."

## LAUREL'S TIPS FOR IMPLEMENTING THE ISTE STANDARDS

When I talk to fellow educators about the ISTE Standards, I begin by trying to put them at ease. The first thing to know is that these standards are non-evaluative and are not content-based. They are meant to help us in our educational practices. ("Yay! The ISTE Standards are your friend!" says Karalee).

There are five sets of ISTE Standards; they all build and interweave common themes and topics in education, but which one(s) you use are dependent upon your role. The five sets of ISTE Standards are:

+ ISTE Standards for Students
+ ISTE Standards for Educators
+ ISTE Standards for Education Leaders
+ ISTE Standards for Coaches
+ ISTE Computational Thinking Competencies

I encourage educators to begin with either the Student Standards or Educator Standards, both of which clearly connect to learning and teaching practices. Each broad standard has multiple indicators that provide definitions and clarifications for the standard. These indicators are the heart of the roadmap and keep us driving on the right educational road toward positive student learning outcomes.

You may be asking yourself, "But what do I do with the ISTE Standards?" I often tell educators to start with a single standard and read and reflect on that standard and all its indicators. Your reflection should be focused on what this standard means to you as you design learning opportunities for your students. Where can you identify that you are on the right road? This is an important reflection question for educators because it can show you that much of what you are doing is already in line with great practices and pedagogy. Conversely, where do you find yourself asking questions or digging deeper into your practice? Reflection is not intended to identify what you are doing wrong, but rather to shine a light on opportunities for growth—for ourselves as professionals and educators, as well as for our students. (Karalee says that Laurel's user-friendly guide through the ISTE Standards can also be used with other standards and frameworks as well.)

1. Choose one ISTE Student or Educator Standard.

2. Read the standard and all its indicators.

3. Reflect on your chosen standard.

4. What does this standard mean to you as you reflect on your own education practices?

5. Where can you identify that you are on the right road?

6. Where can you identify that you can make improvements or adjustments as you design learning opportunities for students?

As the two of us set out to write this book, we wanted to make sure our approach was rooted in solid pedagogy and best practices. Throughout the book, we reference both the ISTE Student Standards and the ISTE Educator Standards where they align with the ideas and practices being discussed. As you read, you will see references to the ISTE Standards and indicators as they are applied to the learning. You can also find all the ISTE Standards at iste.org/iste-standards, along with a host of resources to get you started on your ISTE Standards journey. Happy travels!

> Reflection is not intended to identify what you are doing wrong, but rather to shine a light on opportunities for growth—for ourselves as professionals and educators, and for our students.

## Our Hope for You

This book is the result of a little bit of courage, a friendship, and two women educators willing to ask tough questions. Our insights, as well as our understanding and application of how to use edtech to bring history to life, did not form overnight but are the result of a lifelong journey of iterating, collaborating, and innovating; it's a journey that never ends.

Our hope is that this book will help you make connections and discover practical applications of technology that will enable you to make history come alive for your students. It is vital that students connect empathetically with the past, then apply that lens to the present and future, so that they can learn to be informed, critically thinking, and engaged citizens who care to make a difference in the world. Our mission is to help educators and students demarginalize history so that the diverse, inclusive, full story of history can be brought forth. When students can see themselves as part of history, they can be inspired and motivated to become actively engaged as empathetic, informed people who make a difference *in all their spaces*.

Through this book, we invite you to join our conversation, start from where you are, keep an open mind, and reflect and ask your questions as we embark on this journey together.

Welcome friends,
Karalee and Laurel

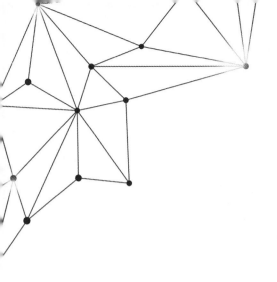

# Part 1

# The Why

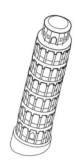

# CHAPTER 1

# The History Chapter

• • • • • • • • • • • • • • • • • • • • • • • • • • • • •

### History Is BORING!
POTENTIALS AND POSSIBILITIES:
AN EXPERIENCE FROM LAUREL

"What exactly is history and why would it matter to thirteen-year-olds?" I began pondering this question from the moment I walked into my new classroom. I was a veteran teacher of thirteen years, but I had previously taught physical and life science, not history or social science. I wanted to move to a school closer to home and to my two children's elementary school, but there were no openings for a science teacher. Instead, I was offered a position teaching U.S. history (which I also had a credential to teach). I jumped at the opportunity. So what if I had never taught the subject? How hard could it be to teach history? Teaching was teaching, right? (Are all the history-social science teachers out there laughing out loud right now?) I was handed classroom keys, a pacing guide for the year's curriculum, a teacher's edition of a ten-year-old textbook, the worksheet masters, and a few reams of paper.

I soon realized that even though I had been a teacher for over a decade, I was certainly not ready for this upcoming school year. Fortunately, two creative and engaging U.S. history teachers from my new department, Kristiane and Courtney, took me under their wing and invited me to collaborate and think outside of the pacing guide with them. I quickly learned to approach teaching history skills through creative project-based learning and inquiry. We used formative assessments to monitor student learning and worked together to improve our teaching practices in the areas that would serve our students best: inquiry, research, critical thinking, argumentative writing, and more. My love of teaching history soared and so did my students' interest in the subject. I was able to regain my hope, recognizing the potential and possibilities that history and civic education could provide for my students.

• • • • • • • • • • • • • • • • • • • • • • • • • • • • • • • • • • • • • •

Why do students say they "don't like history"? Usually, they say it's because history is boring. Who can blame them? Many adults feel the same way when they think back on the history classes they took in school while growing up.

Too often, history has been taught as a list of names, dates, and battles to memorize, or as a celebration of some imaginary glorious past, shining a positive light on only one culture, one state, or one country. And too often, when history is taught this way, students find the subject irrelevant to their lives—and therefore boring. If students don't see themselves as part of the narrative in history or they feel relegated to the literal margins of their textbooks, how can they make connections to civic actions, and how can they make a change in the world? This dysfunctional approach must change; history must be taught in a meaningful way that will provide hope and spark the interest of students, helping them make connections to their learning, as well as to their role as citizens of their school, community, country, and world.

## What Is History?

Dictionaries define "history" as a record of events or the chronological study of human affairs, but there is much more to history than a dry recitation of facts.

History attempts to explain the tapestry of life that came before. We are all part of "history." We are creating it simply by being alive and taking actions in our lives. History matters because we're part of a continuum that started long before we were born and will last long after we're dead. It connects us to the people who came before us and to those who will come after us. But who writes the history, and what do they have to gain by perpetuating myths, stories, and legends? Who is included in the history, and whose stories are left out?

The history we teach needs to be more than a collection of stories or myths. We need instead to examine the real people: their times, societies, choices, and actions that not only shaped their own reality but may also have had lasting impacts on the future.

For example, imagine standing on a road built by the Romans in the fourth century BCE. Who were the people who built these roads? Who were their families, and under what conditions did they find themselves in the position to be constructing these roads? Taking it a step further, how did these roads change the way that the Romans interacted with and expanded their empire? The biggest question of all is this: Why do we still care about all this, thousands of years later? Why do we still teach our students about events that are long past and seemingly without connection to life with cell phones, social media, and Wi-Fi? (Don't worry—there are answers to these questions in the next section!)

We can examine the real people: their times, societies, choices, and actions that shaped not only their own reality but may have had lasting impacts on the future.

## Why Does Teaching History Matter?

It is often said that we study history so that we don't repeat the mistakes of the past. But the purpose of history is more than just avoiding negative repetitive outcomes; a rigorous and engaging history education provides the opportunity for our students to become positive contributors toward our future. Instead of concentrating on avoiding the mistakes of the past, we should be asking: How are we teaching and studying history to learn and grow as people, societies, and as an ever-connected world? Our triumphs and tragedies can serve not only as a reminder of where we come from but also as a guide for where we want to go in the future.

While technology skills are crucial for students to survive and thrive in this digital age, historical thinking skills and historical empathy play a vital role in helping students make connections to their learning, as well as to envision their role as a citizen of their school, community, country, and world.

To develop into informed, engaged citizens, students must learn skills such as critical thinking, creativity, collaboration, communication, and media and technological literacy. The history classroom is uniquely positioned to cultivate those skills because it provides opportunities to:

- promote critical thinking through the study and analysis of primary and secondary sources;
- increase creativity through project based learning and authentic learning opportunities (such as virtual field trips);
- increase communication, helping students to synthesize and express their student voice;
- provide opportunities for students to collaborate and communicate not just with each other, but also through research opportunities (National History Day projects, etc.); and
- supply opportunities for students to examine and evaluate sources to practice media and technological literacy skills.

## WHOSE HISTORY?

"History is written by the victors" (unknown) is a well-known quote, and unfortunately, it has also been the predominant way to teach and learn about history. However, this approach doesn't truly represent history, and it shortchanges our students by failing to provide a complete picture of the past, with all its challenges, failures, and complexities. History must be told through the voices and perspectives of all its stakeholders. Students need to see that history happened to people who looked like them and to people who didn't look like them, to real people who disagreed, debated, collaborated, and worked toward creating the world we live in today. History teachers need to convey to their students that history is full of complexities and nuances, since humans are complex beings.

Dr. Joanne Freeman, an award-winning historian, Yale professor, and leading expert on Alexander Hamilton, says, "History is all about contingencies" (Jones, 2019). There are no guarantees of happy endings, that the "good guys" will always win, that democracy will prevail, and that the nation will stand. There was no magical golden age that came before today. History is full of gray, uncertain areas that need to be examined from multiple points of view. "As much as we might like to, we can't assume that all will be fine in the end. . . . The future is always in flux . . . for better or worse, history doesn't stop. And for that very reason, our actions and decisions now—today—matter in ways that we can't begin to fathom" (Freeman, 2020).

It is imperative that we as educators examine our past and discover the roots of who we are as a people, culture, and society. It is necessary to ask ourselves and our students hard questions: Whose stories are currently being told? Whose stories are being left out (deliberately or not)? Who do we collectively want to be? Asking these questions provides the space for meaningful conversations with students to help them understand their place in the world with the hope of making their present reality more closely match aspirational ideals.

> History must be told through the voices and perspectives of all its stakeholders.

"History Matters (. . .and so does coffee!)" is a weekly webcast sponsored by the National Council for History Education (NCHE). Every Friday morning, Dr. Joanne Freeman, a professor of history at Yale University, discusses a historical topic, what it reveals, and how it connects to people today. After each conversation, she answers questions from the audience. Come join the conversation, learn, ask questions, and have some history fun. You might even see Karalee chiming in the very active "History Matters" video chat (bit.ly/HistoryMattersAndCoffee)!

## HISTORICAL EMPATHY

It is often said that a person needs to understand the past to understand the present, but is that all? What must be done with this understanding? Recognizing where we have come from (as individuals and as a larger society/culture) informs our decisions for today and our perception of possibilities for the future. Educators can foster this process of growth in their students by helping them cultivate historical empathy.

In their article "An Updated Theoretical and Practical Model for Promoting Historical Empathy," Jason Endacott and Sarah Brooks write that historical empathy is a school of thought and/or pedagogical theory to help students look at history through a historical lens of the people and the culture, society, and times that they were living in often through primary sources and contextualization (Endacott & Brooks, 2013).

Students develop historical empathy as they learn the lessons of the past and identify with the real people who made the choices that affect us today. When students can connect the past to the present and have opportunities to apply this empathetic lens to their present world, they learn and practice how to be engaged and informed citizens, both now and in the future.

In "Reflecting the Past, Reflecting the Present: How History is Shaped by Imagination and Perspective," an article published on the website of Harvard's Graduate School of Arts and Sciences, Ann Hall interviews historians on the purpose of studying history in modern times and writes,

> Despite multiple and sometimes conflicting narratives, scholars who study the past provide a window into how our forebears thought and behaved centuries and millennia ago. Often, they discover that we grapple with the same issues, hold the same viewpoints, make the same jokes. We are studying history, but the history of people. People that were living their lives and didn't know how their story would end. . . . In the end, history becomes less about the impossible task of determining what happened at a particular time and more about understanding the multiple dimensions that have influenced people, and how—and why—they continue to have relevance for us today (Hall, 2017).

Teaching both ancient and more recent history benefits students by establishing a chronological understanding of our world timeline, while also expanding students' understanding of the world, cultures, and societies, as well as the changes that occur as civilizations progress and recede. Historical inquiry and empathy are essential parts of any curriculum that is intended to broaden students' understanding of the current world and to incorporate inclusion and diversity into our teaching (Walther, 2018).

Sometimes the past doesn't seem real or relevant to students' lives. They fail to connect with historical figures who exist only in a painting, a black-and-white photograph, or a paragraph in a textbook. Students need to understand that the past isn't made up of esoteric names and faces and random dates and facts. As educators, we need to guide our students into an understanding that history happened to real people (just like them) and that governmental actions and policies have an impact on people in real ways; the positive or negative results still reverberate and affect our lives today and in the future.

Often, history is taught through the lens of "presentism," which means approaching the past from our current perspective. Collectively, societies tend to view and interpret historical events through their own current experiences and culture. This makes it easy to look back and cast judgment on historical events and people. The outcomes of those past events are now known, as well as the ramifications of decisions that people made. A favorite lesson in U.S. history classes is the Age of Jackson; often students are asked to make the case: "Andrew Jackson: Hero or Villain?" This approach to historical teaching can be a useful and necessary scaffold to introduce students to the complexities of history and historical figures. But while it can help students prepare to enter the world of historical inquiry and empathy, we can't let the lessons and learning stop there. We encourage educators to move past the teaching of a simple good-versus-evil, two-dimensional historical world.

When we embed historical empathy and context within content, students can grasp historical foundations and make connections to their lives today. Teaching with historical empathy requires that educators work with students to understand the perspectives of the people who lived before and to examine the personal experiences of the real people who experienced the past and authored historical documents. By infusing historical learning with inquiry and historical empathy skills, students can make connections that will not only impact their historical understanding of the past but will also broaden their understanding of their place in the world and inform how they can actively participate in their communities.

Students develop historical empathy as they learn the lessons of the past and identify with the real people who made the choices that affect us today.

Learn more about historical empathy by listening to "Historical Empathy, Making It Real for Kids," a *Let's K12 Better* podcast conversation between host Amber Coleman-Mortley, podcaster, former teacher, and civic evangelist, and Dr. Katherine Perrotta, Assistant Professor of Middle Grades and Secondary Education with an emphasis on social studies education at Mercer University's Tift College of Education (bit.ly/LetsK12Empathy).

## HEADING DOWN THE ROAD TO BUILDING COMMUNITY

Teaching social studies through the lens of historical empathy may seem like a daunting task, but it is also an exciting opportunity full of potential and possibilities. Before students can authentically connect with the past, teachers need to empathetically connect with them; it all starts with relationships and building community in our classrooms, and we'll talk about that in the next chapter as we head down the road to building community.

# Chapter Wrap-Up

## #TRYONENEWTHINGCHALLENGE

| Getting Started | In the Middle | Deep Dive |
|---|---|---|
| **Self-Reflection** | | |
| Where are you with content?<br><br>How are you providing opportunities for students to explore and "do history"? | How do you encourage and teach historical empathy with your students?<br><br>Where are there opportunities for you to expand historical empathy skills with students? | What history, people, and experiences have been relegated to the margins of the content that is being taught?<br><br>What steps can be taken to make history more inclusive? What voices can be added? |
| **Try One Thing** | | |
| **Project Based Learning Opportunities** | **Explore Historical Empathy Resources** | **Exploring/Attending Content Based Professional Development** |
| Buck Institute/PBLWorks Resources<br><br>bit.ly/BuckInst | Elizabeth Jennings Project<br><br>bit.ly/ElizabethJenningsProject | Gilder Lehrman Seminar<br><br>bit.ly/GilderSeminar |

| Getting Started | In the Middle | Deep Dive |
|---|---|---|
| **Project Based Learning Opportunities** | **Explore Historical Empathy Resources** | **Exploring/Attending Content-Based Professional Development** |
| National History Day<br><br>bit.ly/NationalHD | Facing History Resources<br><br>bit.ly/<br>FacingHistoryResources | Monticello Teacher Institute<br><br>bit.ly/MonticelloMTI |
|  | New Zealand's History Empathy Resources<br><br>bit.ly/NewZealandEmpathy | Ford's Theatre<br><br>bit.ly/<br>FordsTheatreTeachers |
|  |  | OER Project<br><br>bit.ly/ResourcesOER |
|  |  | World History Commons<br><br>bit.ly/<br>WorldHistoryCommons |

## ISTE Standards

- **ISTE Student Standard 1.3 Knowledge Constructor:** Students critically curate a variety of resources using digital tools to construct knowledge, produce creative artifacts and make meaningful learning experiences for themselves and others.

  - 1.3d: students build knowledge by actively exploring real-world issues and problems, developing ideas and theories and pursuing answers and solutions.

- **ISTE Student Standard 1.7 Global Collaborator:** Students use digital tools to broaden their perspectives and enrich their learning by collaborating with others and working effectively in teams locally and globally.

  - 1.7a: Students use digital tools to connect with learners from a variety of backgrounds and cultures, engaging with them in ways that broaden mutual understanding and learning.

 Check out more history resources on our companion website (bit.ly/BringHistoryToLifeHistory1).

# CHAPTER 2

# Community

· · · · · · · · · · · · · · · · · · · · · · · · · · · · · · · · ·

## Resistance and Transformation
### A STORY FROM KARALEE

In late December 2016, my district sent its teachers an invitation to a two-day training on restorative practices. I had never heard of restorative practices before, and this seemed like another one of those initiatives that would probably be dropped by next year, if not sooner. I didn't want to leave my students, but I am a team player, so I dutifully signed up for the training—at least we'd be getting lunch each day. Little did I know that in those two short days, my perspective, my teaching practices, my classroom, and my relationship with my students would be transformed forever.

As the training began, my middle school colleagues and I sat back in our chairs, cynical, daring the trainer to impress us; I was positive I wouldn't speak up or contribute to the conversation. But the presenter was so effective and the message of the importance of building community in our classrooms so compelling that it didn't take long for me to join in. I found myself on the edge of my seat, speaking up and contributing to the discussion. We participated in our own community circle, which taught us the power of building community in our classrooms, and we soon recognized the importance of providing a high level of support and control for students and of listening to and honoring their perspectives and voices.

We practiced fostering student agency by establishing classroom norms together. We experienced how natural and easy it is to check in with our students: "How are you doing? Show us by raising your hand: fist closed (not well) to five fingers (great)." We participated in circle games and learned the fun and power of team building with group juggling, the Wind Blows game, and more. We participated in safe, guided conversations by completing sentence stems after being given time to process and prepare. We also learned about the dividend that building community brings by participating in a fishbowl problem-solving restorative circle.

I returned to my classroom excited and determined to apply what I had learned. Since those two transformative days in 2016, building community has become the priority in my classroom. Every week, with rare exceptions, we circle up, we converse, we connect, we have fun, we listen to each other, and we build community. It has been a game changer that has helped us to navigate the challenges of middle school, tough classroom dynamics, preparation for high school, a fraught political climate, a pandemic, remote and hybrid learning, a destructive TikTok challenge, and more. Community matters.

• • • • • • • • • • • • • • • • • • • • • • • • • • • • • • • • • • • • • •

**Community Circle:** "A circle is a versatile restorative practice that can be used proactively, to develop relationships and build community or reactively, to respond to wrongdoing, conflicts and problems. Circles give people an opportunity to speak and listen to one another in an atmosphere of safety, decorum and equality." (International Institute for Restorative Practices)

- - - - - - - - - - - - - - - - - - - - - - - - - - - - - - - - - - - - -

# Community Circles Games

## THE WIND BLOWS

- What It Is
    - An opportunity for students to move physically and interact with others through community circles.
    - It allows the teacher to strategically sit next to students who could use extra attention during the rest of the community circle.

- How to Do This With Your Class
    - Students are arranged sitting in a circle of movable chairs.
    - One chair is removed from the circle (there is one less chair than the number of students).
    - The student in the middle says, "The wind blows if . . ." Students move if the prompt pertains to them. Students stay in their seats if it doesn't apply to them.
    - Students move across the room to another chair. With one chair missing, one student will end up in the center and will provide the next prompt.
    - Caution: remind students to be respectful and only use prompts that are appropriate; no shaming, etc. Guiding students through a brainstorming activity to generate appropriate prompts is an excellent scaffolding method when first introducing this exercise.
    - Possible examples:
        + The wind blows if you have younger siblings.
        + The wind blows if you had enough sleep last night.
        + The wind blows if you have a test this week.

# GROUP JUGGLING

- What It Is
  - A team building exercise for students.
  - Provides an opportunity for reflection and problem-solving.

- How to Do This With Your Class
  - Students stand in a circle.
  - Students hold up their hands and set the pattern by tossing a soft object to each other, such as a small ball or bean bag. For the pattern, each student will only receive the object once.
  - Once a student receives the object and throws it to the next student, they put their hands down to indicate they've already participated.
  - After the pattern is established, students follow it by throwing the object to each other in the same order.
  - The teacher adds a second object, and possibly more, with the goal to continue the pattern with multiple objects.
  - Debrief with students at the end of the activity:
    - What went well?
    - What did we learn about working together as a team?
    - What could be improved for next time?
    - How can we apply this to other areas in class and in our lives?

# FISHBOWL

- What It Is
  - A way to problem-solve as a class.
  - It should only be introduced and used after the class has connected as a community and a level of trust and respect has been established.
- How to Do This With Your Class
  - Chair setup:

- Three chairs are placed in the middle of a circle of chairs with the teacher or teacher stand-in, one student, and one empty chair for students to rotate through.
- A larger circle of chairs surrounding the center are set up for the rest of the students.
- Routine:
  - Teacher poses a problem or question.
  - Students in the inner circle and the teacher discuss and clarify the problem.
    - If a teacher stand-in is available (could be a student or available adult), then the teacher can go outside of the circle and take notes. If no teacher stand-in is available, the teacher can remain inside the center circle and take notes, or ask a student to take notes. Depending on the problem and classroom dynamic, students may be more willing to speak with a teacher stand-in.
  - Students take turns sitting in the empty chair and offer solutions to the problem or question being posed.
  - Teacher or teacher stand-in listens and then summarizes suggestions.
  - Teacher implements suggestions that may work to resolve the problem or question in the classroom.

- - - - - - - - - - - - - - - - - - - - - - - - - - - - - - - - - - - - - - - - - - -

## Why Community?

"Communities are not built of friends, or of groups with similar styles and tastes, or even of people who like and understand each other. They are built of people who feel they are part of something that is bigger than themselves: a shared goal or enterprise, like righting a wrong, or building a road, or raising children, or living honorably, or worshiping a god. To build community requires only the ability to see value in others, to look at them and see a potential partner in one's enterprise." (Goldsmith, 1993)

The need for a sense of community and belonging is a topic relevant for more than just classroom work or as a foundation for learning. While it is certainly necessary to create community in schools and in classrooms, it is worth looking at how we view community in a macro sense as well. The way we form (or don't form) connections to community as part of a larger society has been the subject of intense speculation and debate. In some sense, it has been a debate of individualism versus the collective whole. In and out of the classroom, we see this manifest itself with a growing lack of trust and empathy toward others.

According to an article by Dr. Patrick L. Plaisance in *Psychology Today*, our connection to a larger sense of society and sense of belonging has grown weaker in recent years, for adults as well as children, and this has been accompanied by a sharp decline in empathy toward others. This lack of trust, empathy, and understanding (even the basic understanding that we don't all have to have the same point of view) can lead to a growing sense of polarization and lack of sense of community in many spaces. This polarization manifests itself in many ways; one example of this in the U.S. is the rise of twenty-four-hour news via cable news outlets. By targeting specific demographics, cable news organizations exploit confirmation bias in their base viewers and profit from a lack of civility and empathy. When people get their news from social media, the danger lies in algorithmic echo chambers that "may limit the exposure to diverse perspectives and favor the formation of groups of like-minded users framing and reinforcing a shared narrative" (Cinelli et al., 2021). Journalists and psychologists alike are conducting research into why people are reluctant to process news empathically and choose instead to stay in their information bubbles to avoid distress and the emotions of guilt or helplessness (Plaisance, 2021).

But there is hope! While we may not have control over echo chambers, algorithms, and cable news outlets, in our classrooms we have a fantastic opportunity to create a sense of community for our students. We can do this by providing time and a safe space to build relationships, where we can get to know each other as people and practice being respectful of and to each other. Providing safe spaces in classrooms for students to practice being good citizens has potential to help them continue these good practices throughout their lives. As educators, our hope is that they will develop into empathetic, respectful citizens whose knowledge and understanding of the past informs their future actions and relationships.

> While we may not have control over echo chambers, algorithms, and cable news outlets, in our classrooms we have a fantastic opportunity to create a sense of community for our students.

--------------------------------------------------

Confirmation bias is our brain's tendency to seek out information that confirms things we already think we know (Common Sense Education, 2021). We all have confirmation bias due to the way our brain chemistry works. In essence, our brain produces the neurotransmitter dopamine, and we feel good every time something that we think to be true is confirmed. Helping students understand confirmation bias can help students understand why it is essential to look at history through multiple perspectives and the historical inquiry process. PBS Learning Media has an excellent lesson on confirmation bias and brain research in their *Above the Noise* series. Check out "Why Do Our Brains Love Fake News?" for resources and an engaging explanatory video (bit.ly/BrainsFakeNews). (We recommend this video for ages thirteen and over; Laurel uses it with adult learners as well.)

--------------------------------------------------

## Why Community Matters in Schools

When we speak of building a community in our classrooms, schools, and beyond, what do we actually mean? "Community" and the broader term "society" are often used interchangeably, but they have different meanings. "Society" can refer to a much larger and heterogenous population that includes many cultures, values, and geographic locations. A community is a supportive social group in which members feel a sense of belonging and share a common interest, experience, or goals (Community Building in the

Classroom, n.d.). Students, like all of us, belong to many communities both in and out of the classroom, as well as larger societies within our states, countries, and world. We in education have the unique opportunity to create a sense of belonging and shared common interest in our classroom communities and to create a safe space for students to participate and form positive student relationships.

The purposeful creation of a safe classroom community is crucial, as positive student relationships are fundamental to learning success and positive educational experiences. This isn't just a pie-in-the-sky, feel-good approach to teaching and learning; it is actually tied to research on how the brain works. Brain science tells us that when students have positive interactions at school, their brains release dopamine. This causes feelings of positivity and engagement in the brain, which lead to a cycle of further engagement and therefore good feelings about school and education. When students feel that they are in a supportive learning environment, they are more likely to have better learning outcomes (Kaufman, 2021).

Intentional community building also helps foster a sense of empathy toward other students. This, in turn, creates a deeper basis for learning: emotional, social, and intellectual support gives students a sense of belonging and of being a part of their classroom community, which fosters an opportunity for them to take ownership and responsibility for their own learning (Community Building in the Classroom, n.d.). It's a classroom community win-win!

> We in education have the unique opportunity to create a sense of belonging and shared common interest in our classroom communities and to create a safe space for students to participate and form positive student relationships.

## How to Build Community in Schools

Building community in our schools and classrooms isn't something that can be forced or just randomly created. In his groundbreaking framework,

Community of Inquiry (COI), Dr. Randy Garrison outlines strategies to build a deep and meaningful learning experience. The framework also outlines three overlapping domains that help create positive learning communities in which students can participate and thrive (Garrison et al., 2000):

1. **Social presence.** Students can feel comfortable being their authentic selves in the learning environment and classroom community.

2. **Cognitive presence.** Students feel that they can learn and provide context and meaning to their learning.

3. **Teaching presence.** The teacher is an intentional leader in instruction and facilitating the growth of the classroom community.

## CONSIDERATIONS FOR BUILDING COMMUNITY

Educators need to consider many factors as they design learning experiences to foster and build a sense of community in the classroom. There is no one-size-fits-most approach; reflection by the teacher is a crucial starting point. Being intentional in designing activities for community building requires preplanning and contemplation of the classroom dynamic, the students enrolled in the class, and what is happening in the school and community at large. There are several steps for teachers to consider before educators begin designing community-building activities:

1. Meet students where they are. To create a safe space for students to be their authentic selves, scaffold activities that build on student participation and comfort levels. Group interactions and activities that are relatively low-risk emotionally (such as the ones described in the beginning of the chapter) can help students feel comfortable and build trust.

2. Remember that community-building activities are not limited to face-to-face interactions. Many students feel more comfortable participating in a classroom community when educational technology is a part of the activities. Edtech can foster a sense of community and belonging while also allowing for learner variability. Some students may prefer activities that can build community via edtech tools, such as creating videos via Flip or posting to a Padlet.

3. Prepare students to participate. In your classroom community, creating norms and expectations encourages participation and builds student ownership of learning engagement and interactions. Include students in the creation of norms to allow for more ownership and buy-in to the classroom community. Other types of support from the teacher may include talking points and sentence frames for peer-to-peer engagement and feedback. Sentence frames provide a structure and support system to encourage rapport-building in a safe environment, and they also provide inclusivity for students who might be learning the language spoken in the part of the world where the classroom is located, as well as adaptability for learner variability (Swartzer, 2019).

The teacher is also a member of the classroom community, and educators should be familiar with their own comfort level with community-building processes. "Going slow to go fast" when building community and being comfortable as the teacher-leader of the community are just as important as norms, activities, and sentence frames.

There is also the question of time: how much time should and can be devoted to community building that goes beyond the beginning-of-the-year "getting to know you" activities that many teachers do with their students? Some educators may be shocked to know that short weekly meetings held with students with the intent to build community may be more effective than long (and often laborious) lessons or activities. When community building is done consistently, with deliberate considerations and intention, it can actually save time because many students will feel part of the classroom community and may be more motivated and connected to the learning process.

**Flip (formerly Flipgrid).** Flip is a safe short-form video tool where teachers can post topics, questions, and more, and students can interact, respond, and demonstrate their learning in creative and engaging ways. This online tool from Microsoft is free and secure for all educators to use with students. Accessibility features such as immersive reader and closed captioning are built into Flip, making it easier for all students to be able to participate and for teachers to see and hear from every student in the class. Flip integrates with Google Classroom and Microsoft Teams and can be shared via QR code and direct link (info.flip.com).

**Padlet.** Padlet is an online digital tool that looks like a digital bulletin board but can do so much more. Teachers can post and share resources with students via Padlet, as well as create Padlets that students can post on. Padlet is a great resource for student collaboration and communication because posts by teachers and students can contain links, videos, images, and document files. The basic Padlet plan is free (as of when this book was published) and, like Flip, integrates directly with Google Classroom and can be shared via QR code and direct links (padlet.com).

## Methods for Building Community

Like Rome, a classroom community isn't built in a day, and the process of building community in a classroom will involve patience and multiple approaches. "Community Building in the Classroom," an article from Columbia University's Center for Teaching and Learning, describes three concrete methods for building community in the classroom:

1. **Icebreakers/Warm-ups.** Short, fun activities designed to foster a sense of community, strengthen social-emotional connections, and help students get to know each other.

2. **Metacognitive Activities and Strategies.** Activities and strategies designed to help students reflect on their own acquisition of knowledge. These activities help students build awareness and a deeper understanding of their own thought processes.

3. **Content-based Activities and Strategies.** These are specific activities and opportunities for student collaboration, based on a particular content area.

## ICEBREAKERS

Icebreakers serve a multitude of purposes when teachers are thinking about community-building practices for their students. Icebreakers should be designed to be quick activities that help build student rapport and help create a positive and collaborative learning community. These activities have the potential to help students feel more connected to their classroom community and therefore open to peer-to-peer collaboration, which fosters a welcoming environment that encourages the sharing of ideas.

1. Design considerations for icebreakers:

   a. Think about the purpose of the icebreaker and what you would like to achieve as part of the classroom community.

   b. Scaffolding, such as providing the question ahead of time or having students respond in pairs or small groups, may help reduce anxiety and prepare students to share with the whole group.

c.  It is important to be considerate of classroom demographics such as the number of students, their familiarity with each other, and other interpersonal considerations.

d.  What is the scope of the activity? Does it require technology? Supplies? Physical space? Don't forget the time factor! (Laurel says, "Always add about ten to fifteen minutes to the time that you think something will take.")

e.  Don't forget to consider student confidentiality, as well as how comfortable students may be sharing personal information. Icebreakers and community circles can be established as a safe space for sharing, but there are educator responsibilities for maintaining student confidentiality and privacy.

f.  Teachers should ask themselves if all students can participate in the icebreaker. Can the activities be adapted for inclusivity and learner variabilities? If not, perhaps the icebreaker can be switched out for a more inclusive option.

g.  Last but not least, it is always important to consider "What to do when . . .?" What happens if things don't go as planned or a student doesn't participate? What if someone comes in late or misses the activity? Patience, having a growth mindset, and modeling flexibility for students are just as important as the activity.

2.  In addition to the activities described at the beginning of the chapter, here are a few more ideas for icebreakers to build community. Keep in mind that teachers may need to start the activity and model it for students at first.

a. "One word" for students to describe themselves. (This can be used in any context. For example, "What is one word to describe how you learn best?")

b. What are six nouns that students can use to describe themselves? (Give students prep time for this before asking them to share.)

c. Create the soundtrack for their life ... so far. Ask students to choose three to five songs that represent an important moment in their life and a short explanation of why that song was chosen. This activity has the possibility of being triggering for some students, so parameters or some examples may be needed, as well as teacher sensitivity.

d. Have students form pairs or small groups and make a list of all the things they have in common.

## METACOGNITIVE ACTIVITIES AND STRATEGIES

Metacognition refers to a student reflecting on their own learning and acquisition of knowledge. This can be a powerful reflection and help students feel empowered in their learning. It can also promote student awareness of their own learning process and that of their peers, which can foster collaboration and community. Shared learning experiences that involve metacognitive processes may help with communication and collaboration within the classroom community.

1. Design considerations for metacognitive activities and strategies:

a. Metacognitive activities and strategies may be new to students. Providing scaffolds to help students process their metacognition is helpful for all learners.

b.  Asking students to share personal learning strategies and participate in group metacognitive activities should only be implemented once they feel safe and part of the classroom community.

c.  Offering multiple ways for students to create, learn, and share with one another with considerations for learner variabilities and inclusivity can help build classroom community.

2.  Ideas for metacognitive activities, strategies, and scaffolds to build community:

a.  Have students reflect on past learning communities: When did they feel happiest in school? The most engaged and respected?

b.  Have students reflect on their personal definition of learning: What does learning mean to them?

c.  Ask questions such as "How do I become a respected human being?" and give prompts such as "I feel the most respected in school when . . ."

d.  Have students write a letter from their future selves, with examples of how they have been successful in their learning in the class/school during the school year.

## CONTENT-BASED ACTIVITIES AND STRATEGIES

By creating specific content area collaborative activities, students can interact and create classroom communities with their peers through shared learning intentions. These activities can also offer students the opportunity to experience working with other students who may learn differently from them.

1. Design considerations for content-based activities and strategies:

   a. It is vital that teachers provide clear instructions, learning intentions, and success criteria for collaborative group work.

   b. Teachers should design opportunities where students collaborate to create expectations and norms for appropriate communication as a classroom community.

   c. Scaffolds such as sentence frames, building on prior knowledge, and checking for understanding can help students with learning and inquiry in the classroom community.

   d. Opportunities for collaborative group reflection can also be combined with metacognitive reflections as part of the community.

   e. As always, teachers must be sure to provide an environment that is inclusive and accounts for learner variability to ensure that all students can participate.

2. Ideas for content-based activities and strategies to build community:

   a. Have students create a soundtrack or playlist for a certain historical event with multiple perspectives represented. (The cast album of the musical *Hamilton* is an example that can be used with students as a model.)

   b. Engage students in brainstorming to connect historically-based vocabulary to current vocabulary. Students can have fun pondering the meaning and context of historical phrases such as "huzzah" or "crapulous" that aren't used today. You can find a fun list on *Time* magazine's website (bit.ly/TimeSpeakFounder). (FYI: "Crapulous" was a favorite phrase of Thomas Jefferson!)

c.  Play games such as "Would You Rather" with historical events/ figures. Students write the questions as the historical figures, then work in pairs or small groups to answer each other.

d.  Watch a short TED Talk or other video together and discuss in a community circle. As a follow-up to the discussion, you could ask students to do a Flip reflection.

e.  Using community circles for check-ins for content-based activities or projects is often helpful to find out how students are feeling about their projects, as well as timelines and clarity of rubrics. This can be valuable formative feedback for teachers and provide an opportunity for adjustments and clarifications if necessary.

**Community Circle TED Talk Video:** "How to Tie Your Shoes" (bit.ly/TedTieShoes). This is a great video to use in circles. After Terry Moore teaches students how to tie their shoes the "right way," he ends with the main point  that "sometimes a small advantage someplace in life can yield tremendous results someplace else." Students discuss the positive benefits of trying something new and discuss how they can apply this to their lives. Going through the process of learning a new way to tie their shoes makes this a lesson they will remember and hopefully apply throughout life.

## Building Community through Historical Instruction

At its core, historical inquiry is the exploration of how groups of people formed communities, cultures, and civilizations (Facing History and Ourselves, n.d.). As we work with students to understand the past through a lens of historical empathy, the natural extension of this is to see how and why people form and dissolve communities. If we help students develop an understanding of the context in which community building happens from a historical point of view, they'll have a basis for making deeper connections to content and to their own communities.

In part 2 of this book, you will find resources, templates, and outlines of lessons that provide opportunities for students to learn historical content and to explore community building through collaboration and historical examples. Some of these lesson plan ideas include:

- **Student Response and Action in Response to Global Migration** (Contributor: Angela Lee)
    - **Overview:** Students engage in a digital journey of Syrian refugees, learn about refugee stories, and design a proposal to help refugees.
    - **Community Connection through Collaboration:** Students learn how their classroom and local communities can understand and create informed civic action plans to respond to a larger global issue.
- **Artifact Investigation** (Contributor: Nathan McAllister)
    - **Overview:** Students engage in historical inquiry through authentic investigations of primary source artifacts.
    - **Community Connection through Collaboration:** Students conduct their investigation collaboratively, either working together as a classroom community or within smaller groups, to analyze, infer, and draw conclusions about their artifacts.
- **The Black Death** (Contributors: Frank Pisi and Barbara Lane)
    - **Overview:** Students will explore historical sources related to the Black Death, learn about its impact during the medieval era, and draw connections to modern-day pandemics.

- **Community Connection through Collaboration:** Through whole-class and small-group discussions, students participate in the classroom community through collaboration. Opportunities to participate in a larger global community exist with extensions to communicate conclusions to the World Health Organization.

## Edtech to Connect

"Global collaboration is necessary to show students that they are part of something bigger than them. That the world needs to be protected and that we need to care for all people. You can show them pictures of kids in other countries but why not have them speak to each other? Then the caring can begin." (Global Read Aloud, 2021)

There are many ways we can harness educational technology to build community within our classrooms and to bring students into the global community. ISTE Student Standard 1.7 Global Collaborator offers a framework for how to approach this: "Students use digital tools to broaden their perspectives and enrich their learning by collaborating with others and working effectively in teams locally and globally."

There are many edtech tools that help foster community building while providing global perspectives and engagement for students, both inside and outside of the classroom. Incorporating global community connections into community building helps students form bridges between all the communities they participate in. It may also open new avenues for students to see themselves as part of a larger global community and give them new awareness and understanding of their place in the world.

- **StoryCorps**
  - **What It Is:** A digital archive of recorded interviews and personal stories that convey the humanity of people from all over the world. "StoryCorps'

mission is to preserve and share humanity's stories in order to build connections between people and create a more just and compassionate world."

- **Global Community Connection:** Students can explore stories from across the country and the world, or they can search for specific stories that correlate with content and projects for the classroom. Students have the opportunity to recognize the global humanity that brings us together, along with perspectives that may be different from their own.

- Flip GridPals
  - **What It Is:** While many teachers and students may already be familiar with creating short-form videos using Flip in their classrooms, there is a unique opportunity to connect with other students and classrooms across the world using Flip GridPals. bit.ly/GridPalsFG
  - **Global Community Connection:** After logging into their teacher accounts, teachers can search and connect with fellow educators from across the world. This allows teachers to collaborate on learning experiences that make connections between their classrooms asynchronously through video (no time zone constraints) in a safe online learning experience.

- Digital Citizenship Institute
  - **What It Is:** The Digital Citizenship Institute's focus is on helping our students connect to the world through our shared citizenship in a digital world. It is all about "humanizing the person next to you, around the world, and across the screen. . . . In today's interconnected world, this is our opportunity to put global education into practice to empower others to become change makers for using tech for good in local, global and digital communities." bit.ly/DigCitInstitute
  - **Global Community Connection:** DigCitKids is one aspect of student engagement and community that is available from the Digital Citizenship Institute. This initiative is focused on

creating digital citizenship opportunities for kids by kids, with a focus on solving real community problems.

+ **Google Earth**
  + **What It Is:** Google Earth is more than just an online map; it also provides resources, lessons, and integrations to be used with students. These include "... step-by-step guides and tutorials on Google's Geo Tools, inspirational stories, plus lesson plans, product information, and much more." bit.ly/GoogleEarthEd
  + **Global Community Connection:** Helping students learn about geography and place gives them a better sense of the world and their place in it. These lessons and resources are varied and help students make connections between people, the land they inhabit, and their impact on it.

+ **PenPal Schools**
  + **What It Is:** Making connections and collaborations with students from dozens of countries across the world allows students to read, write, and create original projects. "PenPal Schools connect students from 150 countries to make friends and discover the world." bit.ly/PenPalConnect
  + **Global Community Connection:** Students can collaborate with students from other countries on projects that matter to them. This is a unique opportunity to not only communicate with students from across the world but also work together on projects with an educational context.

+ **Mystery Skype**
  + **What It Is:** This is a way to build a global community with other classrooms from across the world. It has been described as a global guessing game, in which teachers collaborate and have their classes meet via Skype (or any other online conferencing platform), then have students try to guess each other's location. There are many forms of this Mystery Skype format, and teachers can be creative in their

collaboration to set up the activities (such as only asking the other class yes or no questions). bit.ly/MysterySkypeWhere

+ **Global Community Connection:** With activities such as this, teachers and students connect with classrooms across the world, expand their cultural awareness, and hone their geography skills—while also collaborating as a class to guess the location of the mystery classroom.

+ **Global Read Aloud**

  + **What It Is:** What if your students could read the same book and collaborate with students from across the world? They can! Each year during a six-week period, the Global Read Aloud helps students and teachers connect with resources and activities that are based on a common book. Teachers can connect with other classes from around the world that are participating and decide how much time they would like to dedicate and how involved they would like to be. bit.ly/ReadAloudGlobal

  + **Global Community Connection:** To make these global connections with other classes, teachers can harness the power of edtech to connect using tools such as Skype, Twitter, Padlet, or Flip. "Teachers get a community of other educators to do a global project with, hopefully inspiring them to continue these connections through the year."

. . . . . . . . . . . . . . . . . . . . . . . . . . . . . . . . . . . . .

## Participating in a Global Community— An Experience from Laurel

A few years ago, I taught and advised a group of middle school leadership students. We were swamped with planning activities for our school community, and we also handled the less glamorous business side of the Associated Student Body (ASB), rife with laws, bylaws, invoices, and paperwork galore. Connecting them to a larger global community wasn't even on my radar.

One day, one of my colleagues asked me to look at an email she received. An international charity and education-based organization was looking for school partnerships to get students involved in helping solve global issues. I was intrigued and asked my wonderful student and ASB student secretary, Julianna, to research the organization for our ASB class. The internet came to the rescue, and she was able to find out about the organization, what it represented, and what our potential involvement could be. Julianna was the perfect student for this task. She was studious and fastidious in her online research, and thanks to the inquiry projects in our history class, she knew the basics of lateral reading/researching and finding credible sources. She reported that this was a global charity where the students from our school could actually make a difference in the world—and in a very specific community.

After much discussion and deliberation by the ASB class (with my fellow ASB co-teacher, Marcy, and WEB teacher Andrea), we launched a school-wide campaign to help make a difference in communities around the world. My ASB students devised a fundraising campaign in which each teacher would have a bucket to collect pennies for the charity. Throughout the penny drive, each teacher would receive points for each penny collected, and the ASB students would collect the penny jars, log the amount collected, and store the pennies in a secure location.

The technology needed to run this activity was easy to manage but made a huge difference as my students took their journey into global community work. The students started with easy steps, such as using online spreadsheets to track classroom donations and tally the "winning" classes. Technology tools made it easier to manage the fundraiser and allowed for quick turn-arounds with totals so that every day the students could announce which teachers and classes were in the lead. Cheers reverberated down the halls as the online leaderboard was announced. Imagine our surprise when the loose-change contributions added up to hundreds of dollars, which we were then able to donate to help families in need across the world.

This fundraising campaign built community on many levels: within our ASB class, on our campus, and in the global community. In our ASB class, the students developed a sense of camaraderie as they spoke of how they were able to "make a difference" and "do something real." The school community was brought together as well: teachers from the same wing of the campus who may have only previously waved at each other in the hallway before were now collaborating in an effort to raise the most pennies. They and their classes cheered each other on; there was a true sense of community on the campus. The campaign provided an opportunity for students and teachers alike to understand how they could make a difference.

**Lateral Reading/Searching Online.** Sam Wineburg and the Stanford History Education Group (SHEG) advocate looking at multiple sources and web pages at the same time when conducting an investigation, checking to see if information from one site can be trusted by seeing what other sources say about it. Student researchers are encouraged to open multiple tabs and research "laterally," as opposed to a traditional "vertical search" where they scroll up and down the pages they are evaluating and dig deep into one source at a time. Lateral reading and online searching are important lessons that can help students learn more about historical inquiry and source reliability, as well as develop critical thinking skills that can be transferred to any content area—and beyond the classroom as well (Wineburg, McGrew, 2019). SHEG has other resources and lessons for historical thinking skills (Karalee has adapted and modified the "Lunchroom Fights" lessons for use with her students; you will read more about this in the next chapter). Check out all the resources that SHEG has to offer. stanford.io/35YH9ks

## Heading down the Road to Civics

Students, like all of us, belong to many communities both in and outside of the classroom, as well as in the larger societies within our states, countries, and world. The need for a sense of community and belonging is a topic relevant for more than just classroom work or as a foundation for learning; they are vital components in helping students to understand and see their place and importance in the larger society. And when our students see themselves as members of the larger community and understand the important role they play, they can move from being passive members to active contributors—making a civic connection.

**Penny Drives and Penny Wars.** Conducting a penny drive is fairly easy with online tools such as digital spreadsheets for tracking and doing calculations. The National Parent-Teacher Organization (PTO) outlines how to run a "penny war" with many different variations of rules and ideas on how to effectively host this fundraiser. Ultimately, no matter which rule set a school decides on, it is important to communicate it in a way that builds a shared sense of community with a focus on the ultimate goal of the fundraiser. bit.ly/PTOPennyWars

# Chapter Wrap-Up

## #TRYONENEWTHING CHALLENGE!

| Getting Started | In the Middle | Deep Dive |
|---|---|---|
| **Self-Reflection** | | |
| What are the benefits of building community in your classroom?<br><br>How are you already building community with your students?<br><br>How are you using the study of historical communities to drive conversations about communities today? | How can you further incorporate community building into your classroom in already existing activities?<br><br>How can you further highlight community connections within your content curriculum? | How can you bring global community building into your classroom?<br><br>Where are natural integrations for using edtech for global community student participation? |
| **Try One Thing!** | | |
| Begin to build community with the use of icebreakers. | Plan out and commit to one community circle. | Choose one global edtech community opportunity and implement it with your students. |

Check out more resources for building community on our companion website.

 bit.ly/BringToLifeCommunity2
Bring History to Life Website, Chapter 2

## CHAPTER 3

# The Civics Chapter

· · · · · · · · · · · · · · · · · · · · · · · · · · · · · ·

### Coffee, the Courts,
### the Council, and Civics
#### AN EXPERIENCE FROM KARALEE

During a "Coffee With the Principal" gathering at my middle school, a supportive parent and active community member, MJ, approached me while holding our local newspaper. I teach in a small city with a population of just under 60,000, and MJ told me that our city council had voted to get rid of the only public basketball courts in the city. Even worse, one of the city council members had made derogatory comments about the "type" of people the basketball courts attracted, implying they were undesirable. News outlets including CBS News had picked up the story, and furious citizens were planning to protest at city hall. MJ talked about civic engagement and how this controversy offered students the chance to be in "the room where it happened," and enthusiastically urged me to share this real-life civics lesson with my students.

I set aside the lesson I had prepared for my students. Instead, I played a news video that showed the city council member's comments in his own voice. I also shared the newspaper article, and we then discussed the situation, the facts, and the people interviewed. I asked the students whose voices were missing from these sources, and I reminded them how we always need to consider various sources and points of view. To help them evaluate the evidence and the reliability of sources, I adapted "Lunchroom Fights" from SHEG (Stanford History Education Group) *Reading Like a Historian* lessons. I also mentioned that students would be allowed to make comments to the city council during the upcoming meeting.

On the evening of the city council meeting, protesters outside were handing out signs reading, "I'm the basketball type." I entered the chamber and sat next to a friendly elderly man and a woman, who both expressed concern that the city had not fully informed them about the plans for the park. The man had a folder full of city notices and other paperwork pertaining to the hearing, ready to present when it was his turn. I was impressed to see he was using evidence; it made my history-teacher heart happy.

In an impressive show of civic engagement, a diverse group of residents spoke in favor of the courts. One of my students, Aryamaan, shared a well-prepared, well-thought-out statement in favor of the basketball courts, which he presented with basketball in hand. I was proud to witness him exercising his civic muscle.

The day after the city council meeting, I presented another lesson, using sources loosely based on the meeting. The students studied the evidence and evaluated which sources were the most reliable, a practice our real-life city council members needed to do as they reconsidered the basketball courts controversy.

After the lesson, I described what happened at the city council meeting and shared a video I took of Aryamaan speaking. Brave and caring, he was a great example of what an active, informed, involved citizen looks like—and I was touched that his classmates clapped for him. At the end of the lesson, I revealed that the city council had changed their vote in favor of keeping the basketball court. It was an exceptional and special experience to be able to share the results of this civic action from start to finish, with a resolution so quick and timely.

Shortly after, the mayor reached out to me and came to speak to all my classes. She participated in the community circle team-building activities in all my classes, then sat with my students in the circle and answered their questions. We learned how much a fire truck costs, that the five city council members take turns serving as mayor, that the homeless are undercounted in our city, and that you only need to press the button once when you'd like to cross the street. I was impressed at how responsive and respectful she was to all my students and their questions. One student even asked if her bus could be scheduled later because she had an after-school class. I was surprised by the question, but the mayor respectfully told her she could talk to the street department. My students learned that government officials can listen to and value student voices.

Most importantly, this incident taught my students how to think critically, how to think like historians, and how to evaluate sources and use evidence to make informed decisions. Thanks to technology—including the SHEG online lessons, the video I was able to capture at the city council meeting, and the other news clips that were available online—I was able to turn this event into an engaging and meaningful lesson that showed my students what civic engagement looks like at a local level. They were able to understand how people's voices matter as they witnessed their classmate's contribution and the local government's response.

• • • • • • • • • • • • • • • • • • • • • • • • • • • • • • • • • • • • • •

As mentioned in the introduction, when we first envisioned this book, we imagined it would be about bringing history to life with technology. But just as with other aspects of lesson design and teaching, we found the need to pause, pivot, reflect, and iterate—the unfolding of historic current events prompted and compelled us to broaden our book's focus. We quickly realized that we needed to address history's role in promoting civics and citizenship. Educational technology is a vehicle that provides new and amazing opportunities to bring history to life while also promoting civics and citizenship for meaningful student learning outcomes and engagement.

This revelation led us to ask ourselves more questions, such as: What should we do as educators? How does teaching citizenship impact educational practices? What does this practice look like as we are intentional about building communities in our classrooms, schools, and beyond? We came to one overarching question that forms the basis of approaching citizenship and civic education: How can we reach our students in meaningful ways to expand their understanding of the challenges and opportunities of both civics and citizenship? We emphasize the word "opportunities" because helping activate our students' civic engagement is a profound and wonderful opportunity. As we explore these themes throughout this chapter, we encourage educators to start where they are, considering their own classroom and school communities.

We admit that citizenship and civics may be intimidating and daunting to teach. The past few years have brought a combination of challenges that educators have never faced before. However, opportunities abound for us as educators to change how we perceive civic and citizenship education and embed it in our classroom and school culture. In fact, upon reflection, many educators may find that they are already doing a great deal with civics and citizenship in their classroom communities. We look at the challenges as an opportunity to bring history to life and to cultivate informed and empathetic citizens. Change our civics approach, change our students' perspective, change the world!

## Defining Citizenship and Civic Education

"Nothing could offer higher promise for the future of our country than an intelligent interest in the best ideals of citizenship, its privileges and duties, among the students of our common schools." (T. Roosevelt, 1904)

With a task so critical before us, we needed a deeper understanding of how to define citizenship and civics, as well as how to make them accessible.

The word "citizen" can be intimidating and confusing. We bring all our experiences and biases to our responses and feelings about this word. A multitude of questions arise when we consider this word. What is a citizen? How does the dictionary define this term? Who is a citizen? What are the rights and responsibilities of a citizen? How do we as individuals and as a society understand these terms?

In *A Blog for Civic Renewal*, the philosopher and educator Peter Levine wrote, "You are a citizen of a group (regardless of your legal status) if you seriously ask: 'What should we do?'" (Levine, 2014). This definition resonated with us on many levels. Not only does this definition make citizenship more inclusive, but it also makes it more accessible for educators who may feel as overwhelmed by defining and implementing civic education as we did. This broad definition welcomes all people to participate in the community, regardless of legal status. We are all citizens of the various spaces we inhabit. We are citizens in our home, our classrooms, our school, our communities, our country, and the world. We are all citizens who can ask "What should we do?" in all of these spaces.

What about "civic education"? While researching this book, we identified a few ideas and composite definitions that stood out and resonated with us. One of our favorites came from the *Stanford Encyclopedia of Philosophy*, which defined civic education as "all the processes that affect people's beliefs, commitments, capabilities, and actions as members or prospective members of communities." This powerful definition takes civic education to another level of involvement and is inclusive of all current members of a community, as well as its future members.

Civic education involves engaging and meaningful civics lessons taught in the classroom; it also involves how a school is run. When administrators, staff, and teachers model civic responsibility in their daily interactions, they help create a culture of civic learning through the school systems/ structure. It is crucial to ensure that all students, staff, and other community stakeholders are included in the operations of a school because this is a powerful way for students to learn about the possibilities of civic engagement. "Students learn much more from the way a school is run," comments Theodore Sizer, "and the best way to teach values is when the school is a living example of the values to be taught" (Crittenden, 2018).

Schools convey powerful and important lessons that go far beyond the curriculum and standards. As educators, we must seize this opportunity to help students define their understanding of what citizenship and civics mean to them as members of multiple communities—both now and later in their lives.

How can we reach our students in meaningful ways to expand their understanding of the challenges and opportunities of both civics and citizenship?

- - - - - - - - - - - - - - - - - - - - - - - - - - - - - - - - - - - - - - -

## iCivics—Emma Humphries

Both Laurel and Karalee are proud members of the iCivics Educator Network—a community dedicated to promoting "high-quality equitable civic education." As we wrestled with our understanding of citizenship, Karalee asked, "Why don't we talk to Emma?" Dr. Emma Humphries is the chief education officer for iCivics, Inc. and the deputy director of CivXNow. In our conversation, Emma offered many insights regarding the possible definition of citizenship and civics, and she also introduced us to the expanded definition of "citizen" offered by Peter Levine. bit.ly/iCivicsEd

Laurel and Karalee's students, as well as thousands of other students across the nation, have benefited from and enjoyed iCivics resources; they especially love playing the engaging educational games such as *Do I Have a Right?*, *Executive Command*, and *Win the White House*, to name a few. (Teachers love playing these games too; check out Twitter to find history-social science and civics teachers showing off their iCivics game scores!) Dr. Humphries' tip for motivating students and upping the stakes with iCivics games is for the educator to play the game first, earn and share their high score, then challenge students to beat their score. It's an excellent strategy for student engagement.

iCivics, Inc. is a nonprofit educational provider founded by former U.S. Supreme Court Justice Sandra Day O'Connor to promote "equitable, non-partisan civic education so that the practice of democracy is learned by each new generation . . . by providing high quality and engaging civics resources to teachers and students" in the United States.

CivXNow is "a national cross-partisan coalition of over 100 organizations focused on improving" K–12 civic education in the United States. civixnow.org

---

## Revitalizing the Teaching of Civics

For a long time, civics has been put on the educational backburner in the United States. According to Educating for American Democracy (EAD), U.S federal spending on STEM education in recent years was approximately $50 per student, while civic education received only five cents per student (Swann, 2021). No Child Left Behind in 2001 and Educate to Innovate in 2009 both focused on improving student learning outcomes in reading, science, and math content areas. In both pieces of legislation, there is a noticeable lack of emphasis on history, social science, and civic education (Burke & Baker 2011).

Not surprisingly, recent studies have indicated that civic knowledge and public engagement in civics in the United States may be at an all-time low. In 2016, the Annenberg Public Policy Center found that only 26% of Americans could name all three branches of government. In an article written for The Center for American Progress, the authors state, "Without an understanding of the structure of government; rights and responsibilities; and methods of public engagement, civic literacy and voter apathy will continue to plague American democracy. Educators and schools have a unique opportunity and responsibility to ensure that young people become engaged and knowledgeable citizens" (Shapiro & Brown, 2018).

Fortunately, there is now a resurgence in interest in civic education. A Pew Research Center Charitable Trust article from May 2021 describes how lawmakers in at least thirty-four states have debated eighty-eight bills that seek to increase civic education in public schools. These measures range from mandating civic education for middle and high school students to creating incentives for students to participate in civic activities outside the classroom (Vasilogambros, 2021).

*Do I Have a Right?* by iCivics is a fast-paced and engaging gamification of learning where students run and manage a law firm that specializes in constitutional law. This is a U.S.-focused game that is a great way for students living in the U.S. to apply what they have learned about the U.S. Constitution and the Bill of Rights, at the end of a unit or for U.S. Constitution Day. It also may be a way for students outside of the U.S. to learn about another country's system of government and constitution. bit.ly/HaveARight

### EXPLORING GLOBAL CITIZENSHIP

The desire to reintroduce civic education into the school curriculum is not unique to the United States. In 2017, the Chilean Ministry of Education proposed legislation to incorporate citizenship education as a mandatory course for students in the final two years of their secondary education (Zúñiga et al., 2019). Based on the groundwork laid by the United Nations Universal Declaration of Human Rights, UNESCO has further expanded with the Global Citizenship Education initiative. This initiative aims to "empower learners of all ages to assume active roles, both locally and globally, in building more peaceful, tolerant, inclusive and secure societies." (United Nations, 2020) This, in combination with #4 of the United Nations Sustainable Development Goals (SDG), Quality Education, aligns with the ISTE Educator Standard 2.2b: "Advocate for equitable access to educational technology, digital content and learning opportunities to meet the diverse needs of all students." This truly is an international movement to reincorporate citizenship and civic education back into mainstream educational curriculum across the globe.

The 17 Sustainable Development Goals (SDGs) adopted by the United Nations in 2015 urge all countries to work together to end poverty, protect the planet, and ensure peace and prosperity for all by 2030. If you are interested in learning how you can bring the SDGs into your lessons and curriculum, check out *Teach Boldly: Using Edtech for Social Good* by Jennifer Williams. You can also learn more on Twitter (of course!) by following the hashtag #TeachSDGs. iste.org/TeachBoldly bit.ly/17SDGoals

## "What Should We Do?"

According to an article from the Brookings Institution, there are several ways that we can approach teaching civic education:

1. **Civic knowledge and skills**

2. **Civic values and dispositions**

3. **Civic behaviors**

If built upon, these foundational skills can lead students from knowledge acquisition to engaging in positive civic behaviors (Winthrop, 2020). It is important to note that students and teachers alike need to develop these skills. In this next section, we'll take a deeper look at each of these foundational skill areas, as well as examples of activities and resources that can help develop them in the classroom. As you read the list, we suggest you reflect on what you are already doing with your students, then ask yourself: Where can I go next?

1. **Civic knowledge and skills.** Baseline knowledge can help students form a foundational understanding of government processes, political philosophies, constitutional rights, and civic responsibilities, as well as important historical background and inquiry skills.

    a. Teach civic structures and history of the country

    b. Look at citizenship tests from around the globe

    c. Examine country-specific documents and historical foundations (for example, the U.S. Constitution and Bill of Rights and the United Nations Universal Declaration of Human Rights)

2. **Civic values and dispositions.** Teaching students to gain an understanding of civil dialogue, free speech, and understanding multiple perspectives

or points of view is crucial for building upon knowledge acquisition. Student inquiry and participation in active learning strategies helps solidify the learning, as well as make it more relevant to students.

    a.  Project based learning

    b.  Mock trials

    c.  National History Day projects

    d.  Philosophical Chairs exercise

    e.  Socratic seminars (Deep Dive teachers!)

3.  **Civic behaviors.** Helping students to develop agency with civics to participate, volunteer, and engage with their communities is how we can help them look at civics and citizenship through their own lens and make personal connections to their community and beyond.

    a.  School elections and activities

    b.  Community and school board meetings

    c.  Community events (volunteer or attend)

    d.  Partnerships with community organizations

    e.  For older students, this may include pre-registering to vote or voting

Taking the time for self-reflection and looking for ways that civics is already being incorporated into the curriculum is a great place to start when thinking about lesson design, student activities, and demonstration of learning.

Civics can be the lens through which educators look at the curriculum and design learning activities throughout the school year. The opportunities for integrating civics into meaningful student learning makes it not "one more thing," but the basis of understanding and teaching history.

 bit.ly/PhilChairs
Philosophical Chairs is a structured discussion method that promotes critical thinking and dialogue in the classroom. Students respond to a question or debatable topic, then are given the opportunity to provide evidence and change their minds. Scan the corresponding QR code to check out this short video from Julie Thoms on how to structure effective Philosophical Chairs. For those teachers who want to take structured discussion methods to the next level after their students have mastered Philosophical Chairs, Socratic seminars are a natural progression. Check out an article from Edutopia on Socratic seminars using the QR code. edut.to/3pIJA1S

The opportunities for integrating civics into meaningful student learning makes it not "one more thing," but the basis of understanding and teaching history.

Project based learning (PBL) is an approach to teaching and learning in which students engage in a project that addresses a real-world problem or meaningful challenge. PBLWorks defines a "gold standard" of project design as consisting of seven essential elements; one of the seven is "inquiry," which makes PBL an excellent extension of the historical inquiry essential to the social studies curriculum. Check out the resources available for educators at PBLworks.org.

## Having a Civics Mindset

Often, civic and citizenship education is looked at as a stand-alone unit or lesson. Time is always a factor, and educators have other standards and content that also need to be taught. However, civics and citizenship can be embedded into all content areas by creating a culture and intentionality of civic-mindedness in the classroom. This long-lasting and effective approach is to infuse civics into everything, from creation of class rules and norms to a larger approach to projects and deeper understandings. For many educators, a starting point can be to look at classroom curriculum and identify places where civics and civic discourse are already being taught, and then look for areas that can be added or built upon.

For example, at the start of the school year, teachers can build community by including students in conversations about how to establish classroom norms. Taking it a step further and inviting students to discuss what norms look like outside of the classroom can lead to interesting and meaningful civic conversations. Asking questions about how norms are established for the school, the community, the state, and the nation can spark conversations about civics and lay the foundations for deeper inquiry as the year progresses.

Another easy entry point for starting civic conversations could be speaking to students about school-based activities, such as school spirit days. Asking questions such as, "Who creates these activities, why are they created, who benefits from them, why should a person participate, and how can they be more inclusive?" can lead to powerful conversations about civics and school citizenship. Helping to establish a mindset of citizenship and civics through low-stakes activities and questions can lead to powerful learning opportunities and further connections, as well as further community building in the classroom.

> Classroom norms are the spoken and unspoken rules that help students understand how to navigate the classroom environment, as well as their place in it (Finley, 2014). Norms are not just a rule set that a teacher creates; we encourage you to check out this article from Edutopia on the science behind classroom norms and some ideas for developing substantial norms that both benefit students and help establish the classroom environment. edut.to/3sR4i1r

## DIGITAL CITIZENSHIP

As we write this chapter, a disturbing social media trend has directly affected students and schools and highlights the need for civic education in many forms in our classrooms and schools. TikTok is a social media platform known for short-form videos. Users of TikTok often pose each other challenges to be filmed and then followed with a hashtag. A TikTok trend that hit schools in late 2021 was called the "devious lick" challenge. To "lick" is to successfully steal something; the more outrageous the "lick," the more "devious" it was considered. This challenge started with students stealing from teachers and destroying school restrooms, all while filming themselves and posting it publicly on the TikTok platform. The trend became popular, with millions of views from TikTok users, and it showed the disconnect that students felt toward school, their teachers, and their campuses. bit.ly/TikTokLicks

Why would students film themselves committing acts of theft and vandalism and posting them publicly? TikTok banned the hashtag and pulled down any videos associated with it, but the damage was done. Public outcry resulted in calls for students to be punished, for guards to be posted outside restrooms, for schools to have students sign in and out for restroom use, and more. Threats of suspension, restitution, and expulsion were advertised to parents and students alike. What wasn't addressed was the correlation between being a good citizen (not vandalizing and stealing from school) and being a good digital citizen (not posting said vandalism on the internet for all to see as part of the student's digital footprint).

As our world has become increasingly digitized (we are writing this book on laptop computers, connected to Wi-Fi, on a shared online document that is housed in the virtual cloud), the line between "citizen" and "digital citizen" has been blurred to the point of nonexistence. Everything is global now, from our capability to bury ourselves in the twenty-four-hour news cycle and updates on popular social media sites, to students posting short-form videos of themselves engaging in destructive behaviors. Digital citizenship was once thought of as predominantly "digital safety": How can we keep our students safe from online predators, phishers, and hackers? Those ideas are still important and should be included in all education. However, as the "devious lick" trend makes clear, students also need a foundation in being not only careful and responsible consumers of social media but also responsible creators of digital content.

Like citizenship and civics, digital citizenship is often looked at as "one more thing" that overworked and exhausted teachers need to incorporate into their already full curriculum. But it doesn't have to be one more thing: Creating a culture of citizenship lends itself to including digital citizenship in the conversations as well. Speaking to students about TikTok trends and digital footprints and having students participate in creating norms for online student interactions and collaborations can set the stage for integration of digital citizenship lessons or further integration of digital citizenship into content areas and classroom communities.

One place to start is the ISTE Standards. As we mentioned in the introduction to this book, the ISTE Standards are a roadmap for educators to follow and use as a guide and pedagogical foundation for teaching and learning practices. In both the Educator Standards and the Student Standards, digital citizenship is addressed directly. ISTE Educator Standard 2.3 outlines how educators can build a culture of responsible digital citizenship: "Educators inspire students to positively contribute to and responsibly participate in the digital world." ISTE Student Standard 1.2 focuses on digital citizenship from the perspective of students: "Students recognize the rights, responsibilities and opportunities of living, learning and working in an interconnected digital world, and they act and model in ways that are safe, legal and ethical." It is well worth the time for educators to refer to the ISTE Standards and use their indicators as a checklist for reflection on where they are hitting the mark and where improvements could be made.

As you look for ways to embed digital citizenship as part of your classroom culture, you may want to approach "DigCit" through self-reflection, as well as a growth mindset. Teachers don't have to know about every new app or trend, but they can reflect on how they are personally modeling digital citizenship and media literacy for their students.

You can find out more about digital citizenship and meaningful ways to create a culture of DigCit in your classroom through *Digital Citizenship in Action: Empowering Students to Engage in Online Communities,* a wonderful book by our fellow ISTE author Dr. Kristen Mattson. This user-friendly introductory book provides guidance and practical ways for building community in digital spaces both in and out of the classroom. iste.org/DigCitAction

Teachers don't have to know about every new app or trend, but they can reflect on how they are personally modeling digital citizenship and media literacy for their students.

## Digital Citizenship and Civics through Edtech

It's important to make connections between citizenship and digital citizenship for our students both inside and outside their learning environment. Digital citizenship isn't limited to school computers or projects; it applies anytime students engage in a digital space or community. Teachers can extend the dialogue by making connections to students as global digital citizens who are both consumers and contributors.

Best of all, teachers don't have to navigate these digital citizenship waters alone. There are plenty of robust programs and curricula out there that can help students connect to civic engagement, content area learning, and digital citizenship. It is important to remember that digital citizenship *is* a part of citizenship and can easily be included in your civics curriculum and instruction.

There are a vast number of digital citizenship and civics resources available online. A starting point for educators may include:

+ iCivics

> How do we get students excited to learn about civics and foundational governmental structures? Gamification! iCivics offers educational online games with accompanying lesson plans and

resources to promote engaging civic education, as well as encourage students to become active citizens (icivics.org).

+ Common Sense Education

    Common Sense Education is a nonprofit educational organization that is dedicated to providing free digital citizenship resources for educators to use with their students. Resources are grade-level specific and align with the ISTE standards, Common Core ELA standards, American Association of School Librarians, and CASEL (Collaborative for Academic, Social, and Emotional Learning) framework (commonsense.org).

+ We the Civics Kids (Constitution Center)

    The Constitution Center offers a series of lessons that teaches students about the election process and encourages them to be active citizens in their classroom, school, home, and community. Resources include monthly curated lists with recommendations for resources with an emphasis on civics in literature and primary source/historical texts (bit.ly/CivicsKids).

+ Smarthistory

    Art history is a powerful way to combine visual and performing arts with world history for students. Smarthistory is an excellent means for students to access art history as all their resources are available under a Creative Commons non-commercial license and free to use. The "Seeing America" section is called a "portal to American art and history." These resources were curated from collections from seventeen leading U.S. museums and are categorized by theme, historical periods, and classroom topics. Educator guides and resources make using this with students engaging and easy to implement (smarthistory.org).

+ The Living Room Candidate

    Pop culture is another accessible way to examine the history and civic culture of a community or country. The Living Room Candidate hosts a collection of more than 300 commercials from every U.S. presidential election since 1952. The 2020 edition of the Living Room Candidate was supported in part by the National Endowment for the Humanities: Exploring the Human Endeavor. Lessons and resources have been created for use by secondary teachers and students and align with Common Core State Standards (bit.ly/LivingRoomCan).

+ The Ronald Reagan Presidential Foundation and Institute

The Reagan Foundation, part of the Reagan Presidential Library (located in Southern California), has developed a curriculum that focuses on civics and citizenship through the use of primary source materials. An online learning hub offers resources such as virtual field trips and tours for students from all over the world. The library also offers engaging, immersive role-playing experiences both in person and virtually. Check out the Airforce One Discovery Center and The Situation Room Experience for a highly engaging, immersive, educational experience (bit. ly/ReaganFoundation). (See sidebar.)

+ Composer Education

Composer Education offers thousands of curated resources on a wide range of topics, including civic learning, social justice, social-emotional learning, and global competencies. Support for teachers includes research-based tools and guidance for curriculum planning to tailor learning experiences for students in specific content areas and curriculum (composereducation.org).

+ DigCitCommit

Curated from reliable and trustworthy sources from across the globe, DigCitCommit helps bring the best digital citizenship resources to teachers and students. The heart of DigCitCommit focuses on the five DigCit Commit competencies: inclusive, informed, engaged, balanced, and alert. These competencies are designed to focus less on what students shouldn't do and more on taking a proactive approach that challenges students to stay safe, become problem solvers, and spread positivity online (digcitcommit.org).

◆ CyberWise

A major part of being a student in the digital age is gaining the knowledge and skills to become a safe and discerning creator of online content and consumer of technology. CyberWise has resources to help educators, administrators, and parents integrate digital citizenship into their classrooms, after-school programs, and homes (cyberwise.org).

Teachers don't have to navigate these digital citizenship waters alone.

The Reagan Library's Air Force One Discovery Center and the Situation Room Experience are highly engaging, immersive, edtech role-playing experiences that challenge students to use their critical thinking and problem-solving skills while collaboratively working under pressure to make decisions, iterate, and adapt as a fast-paced scenario unfolds. In the Air Force One Discovery Center, students role-play as presidential advisors, military officials, or members of the White House press corps. In the Situation Room Experience, high school and university-level students face a modern-day U.S. constitutional crisis as members of the president's cabinet and as members of the news media.

Note: Though these immersive experiences are housed at a U.S. Presidential Library, they are not partisan-based experiences. Karalee's students have participated in both experiences, and she has seen firsthand that this is an amazing way to bring history to life with edtech.

These experiences are not limited to Southern California, where the Reagan Library is located; there are other virtual and in-person immersive experiences at other presidential libraries and beyond. Mount Vernon, the home of America's first president, George Washington, hosts the Situation Room Experience: Washington's Cabinet.

## Conclusion

Part 1 of this book has been a journey through the "why" of historical thinking, teaching, citizenship, and civics. We have taken a deep dive into the educational basis and importance of history, community, and civics in our social studies classrooms. In each chapter, we have encouraged you to reflect on your own journey and to "try one thing!"

Now is a great time to top off that beverage that we encouraged you to pour in the introduction (tea, coffee, Diet Coke, Cherry Coke . . . whatever you'd like!) and join us for part 2, where we will move into the "how" and help you bring history and civics to life for your students using edtech tools and resources. We will also share lessons created by award-winning educators that you can use right away or adapt to your own classroom curriculum. Cheers!

## Chapter Wrap-Up

| Getting Started | In the Middle | Deep Dive |
| --- | --- | --- |
| **Self-Reflection** | | |
| How do you define citizenship and civics for your students? | Reflect on "the How": Civic knowledge and skills, civic values and dispositions. | Review and reflect on ISTE Standards for Educators. |
| **Try One Thing!** | | |
| Identify how you are already integrating citizenship and civics into your curriculum. | Choose an area of focus to integrate into your student learning activities. | Choose one of the resources from the Digital Citizenship and Civics through Edtech section to use with your students. |

Check out more resources for building cultivating engaged citizens on our companion website.

 bit.ly/BringToLifeCivics3
QR_3.15 BringToLifeCivics3
Bring History to Life Website, Chapter 3

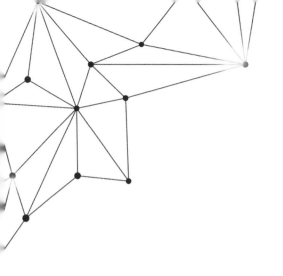

# Part 2

# The How

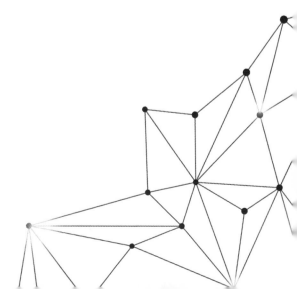

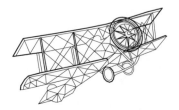

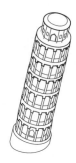

# CHAPTER 4

# Edtech to Connect

· · · · · · · · · · · · · · · · · · · · · · · · · · · · · · · · · · · ·

### An Experience from Laurel

"Mrs. K! You have gotta get over here!" I had taken my eighth-grade class to the computer lab, and now I had a student frantically waving her hand in the air and whisper-yelling to call me over.

When I first told my students we were going to search online databases–such as the U.S. National Archives and Library of Congress–for primary sources for their National History Day projects, my enthusiasm was met with collective groans and stares. Now I was concerned as I navigated my way through the sea of backpacks on the floor and quickly made my way over to see my student pointing emphatically at her screen.

On her computer screen, I could see that she was researching on the U.S. National Archives website. An image of a blue-tinged telegram filled the screen. As I looked closer, I could see that this was a primary source artifact–one of the actual telegrams Jackie Robinson sent to President Lyndon B. Johnson in 1965 had been scanned and uploaded for viewing (Robinson, 1965). I asked her what was going on, and she replied with a question. "Did you know that Jackie Robinson didn't just play baseball!? He was also really involved in the civil rights movement. He sent telegrams to the president!"

Now that my students could see history for themselves—the artifacts, news clippings, telegrams, and more—through their computer screens, their response to "seeing history" began to match mine. Their enthusiasm and excitement over finding relevant primary sources online was so much more than my teacher's heart could have ever hoped for. It was one thing for me to show my students primary sources in my classroom, but for a student to discover them for themselves, make connections to history, *and* see themselves in history was so much more powerful. The next time I announced that we were having a research day in the computer lab, their response was much more enthusiastic.

· · · · · · · · · · · · · · · · · · · · · · · · · · · · · · · · · · ·

> It was one thing for me to show my students primary sources in my classroom, but for a student to discover them for themselves, make connections to history, *and* see themselves in history was so much more powerful.

The U.S. National Archives has many resources that can be easily accessed by both teachers and students. While students can dig into the archives and see what primary source materials have been digitized through an easy-to-use search tool, teachers can visit the educators' section. Within this section, teachers will find resources such as "We Rule: Civics for all of U.S.," a free distance learning education initiative that provides teachers with programming, curriculum, and virtual field trips. Teachers will also find DocsTeach, a resource repository with thousands of primary sources, including letters, photographs, and videos, along with document-based activities and lessons created by experts from the Archives and by teachers from around the world. archives.gov

Teaching is an art. Educators are creative in designing engaging lessons, assessing student understanding, engaging in feedback loops, and more. Teaching is a challenging and demanding job with educators constantly working to be successful collaborators and problem solvers. Truly, being an educator is not for the faint of heart.

Educational technology (edtech for short) isn't just about the latest or best new tool that has hit the market (or your inbox). Remember when overhead projectors and TVs outfitted with the newest in LaserDisc technology made the new tool list? (No? Oh . . . us, neither!) Edtech should be used in the classroom to support your instruction and expand what you are able to do (Farah & Arnet, 2019). It is essential to select edtech that is relevant to your content material to help make it come to life for students. Edtech used for the sake of using it has the potential to have the opposite effect on students; they can become overwhelmed and not make the connections to learning. This chapter will make clear how to use educational technology in meaningful ways that expand on historical learning and civic education, as well as explore what not to do.

National History Day (NHD) is historical project based learning at its finest. National History Day is an educational program that also happens to be a contest. Each year, National History Day releases a new historical theme for students to engage in historical inquiry. The theme provides a historical lens through which students can research and engage with primary and secondary sources. Each theme is purposely broad so that it can be applied to national, state, or world history, and it has relevance to ancient history as well. Past themes include Triumph and Tragedy in History, Conflict and Compromise in History, Taking a Stand in History, and more. (Laurel likes to use the annual NHD theme as her essential question for the school year because it applies to all history-social sciences content area topics.) After students conduct their research, they can communicate their findings in a variety of ways, including creating an exhibit, website, documentary, performance, or paper. You can find out more at NHD.org.

Edtech provides an opportunity to support both teachers and students. With the influx and explosion of new educational technology over the past ten years, it can easily be overwhelming to decide what edtech to introduce into the classroom and curriculum. Teachers need to be aware of which edtech applications (apps) and websites have been approved by their district for use with students. Student data privacy and concerns over the security of students' personally identifiable information (PII) is a major issue and has been identified in several federal laws (see the FERPA and COPPA sidebar). A good practice is to always check with your IT department when thinking about introducing new educational technology into use with students.

It is essential to select edtech that is relevant to your content material to help make it "come to life" for students.

- - - - - - - - - - - - - - - - - - - - - - - - - - - - - - - - - - - - - - - - - - - - - - - - -

Student data privacy (SDP) is important for all students, and protecting it is the law in the United States. FERPA and COPPA are acronyms for U.S. laws that are meant to protect a student's  privacy when it comes to their education and educational records. Many countries around the world have similar policies, but as we (Laurel and Karalee) are U.S.-based, we will highlight these two laws. You can find more information and examples of SDP laws from countries around the world below. bit.ly/FERPAprotect

FERPA stands for the Family Educational Rights and Privacy Act, a U.S. federal law that is meant to protect the privacy of a student's educational records and provides families with protection and choices about what information is shared about their student.

This law is important for U.S. educators and applies directly to educational technology that may be used in the classroom. The crux of this law is that students have a right to have their educational records kept private. If you aren't sure what constitutes an educational record for a student under the age of eighteen, think about a student's personal information, such as (and not limited to):

- birth date
- address
- grades earned
- test scores
- classes and/or courses taken
- special education records
- medical/health records

You can find a complete list of what is protected under FERPA from the U.S. Department of Education.

Educational records are often housed in a learning management system (LMS) such as Google Classroom, Microsoft Teams, or Canvas, as well as in apps and online learning platforms that integrate with an LMS. It is the responsibility of the teacher, school, and district IT department to protect a student's educational record.

A vital part of following the law is making sure you protect student data and educational records with passwords and only use online applications that have been approved by the district's IT department for use with students. (A favorite saying of Laurel's is "Always ask before you app!")

COPPA is the acronym for the U.S. Children's Online Privacy Protection Act. This U.S. federal law is aimed at companies that provide websites and apps that may have interactions with children under the age of thirteen. In the U.S., you will often find a digital check for COPPA with a website or app asking a new user if they are over the age thirteen. ftc.gov

How does this apply to schools? School districts are required to ensure that all apps and websites being used with students are adhering to the law, and, if any student information is being collected, it is only for educational purposes and not for commercial use (for instance, records and other information being sold to other companies or children being advertised to through the app).

Both FERPA and COPPA are meant to protect our students and their right to privacy in their education. This is why it is essential for teachers to only use websites and applications that have been vetted and approved by their district or local educational agency (LEA). Teachers may be held liable if they are found to not follow these laws, including having disciplinary action taken at work and possibly even losing their jobs. While this caution may seem extreme, it is truly a case of "an ounce of prevention is worth a pound of cure" as Benjamin Franklin cautioned. He gave his warning in 1735, but it still applies—only now to selecting websites and apps to use with your students and not fire prevention. (Well, maybe firewalls . . . but that may be a stretch!)

Not in the U.S.? As mentioned above, most countries' information regarding SDP can be found readily with a quick internet search. Here are a few that we have researched as international examples (as of the writing of this book):

- Nigerian policies are outlined in the African Academic Network on Internet Policy. bit.ly/AfricanAcademic

- India's concerns for students are addressed in this article from Firstpost. bit.ly/IndiaStudentData

- Read about the European Union Committee for Education's General Data Protection Regulation (GDPR). bit.ly/EUGenDataProtection

- Find out more about Brazil's student data privacy laws in this article located on the website for the Câmara Dos Deputados (Chamber of Deputies). bit.ly/BrazilStudentData

---

A vital part of following the law is making sure you protect student data and educational records with passwords and only use online applications that have been approved by the district's IT department for use with students.

## EdTech to Support *All* Learners

Classrooms are filled with unique learners from different backgrounds and cultures, with diverse needs, capabilities, and learning abilities. According to research from the Pew Institute, it is estimated that one in seven students in the United States—approximately 14% of the currently enrolled student population—has an identified learning disability. While the global number is hard to estimate due to reporting data inconsistencies from various countries, it can be extrapolated that these numbers are not unique to the population of the United States (United Nations, 2020).

Ensuring that all our students have access to free and appropriate education isn't just a wish that we have for our students; it's the law. In 1975, the United States passed the law now known as IDEA (Individuals with Disabilities Education Act), which guarantees every child with a disability access to a free and appropriate public education in the least restrictive environment. Educational technology applications created over the past ten years have brought huge advances that can give students greater access to classroom materials and reduce restrictive environments as well. This commitment to accessibility for all students can be seen in the ISTE Standards for Educators 2.2.b.

**Leader 2.2.b:** Advocate for equitable access to educational technology, digital content, and learning opportunities to meet the diverse needs of all students.

+ **Ensure** all students have access.
+ **Accommodate** for individual student needs.
+ **Advocate** for an **equitable system.**
+ Consider **learner variability, language skills, and technology and internet access.**

This commitment to advocate for equitable access forms the basis of how we can approach accessibility for our students. Often, educators have the best intentions for increasing accessibility for students to class materials, but don't know where to start. There are wonderful guidelines that can also help to reduce barriers to learning and participation for students with disabilities. For example, the National Center on Accessible Educational Materials (AEM) provides resources that can help educators make learning accessible to all students. aem.cast.org

Keep in mind, making lessons accessible doesn't benefit only students with disabilities; it benefits all students, including those with literacy challenges, multilingual students, and more.

## POUR

A great acronym for checking accessibility for presenting materials to students and also teaching them to increase their understanding of accessibility is POUR: Perceivable, Operable, Understandable, Robust. bit.ly/AccessPOUR

- **Perceivable:**
    - Can materials be seen, heard, and observed by learners to acquire content?
        - Speech to text
        - Immersive reader options
        - Consistent color, layouts
        - Font choice
        - Font size

**Start here:** Turn on closed captioning or live transcriptions as much as necessary.

- **Operable:**
    - Can learners interact with the materials as necessary and intended for learning outcomes?
        - Logical progressions with tabs and menus for navigation
        - Linked files are supported with same accessibility provided
        - Check for built-in accessibility checkers available on some tools.

**Start here:** Make sure that headings are used for logical navigation through the material.

- **Understanding:**
  - Is there access for comprehension and understanding for learners using tools or multiple modalities?
    - Content structure
    - Clear titles
    - Headings are clear and not repeated
    - Color is not used for emphasis or meaning
    - Alternative text for images is provided
    - Underlining is only used for hyperlinks, not emphasis

**Start here:** Check how you are emphasizing within text—use bold text instead of underlining or color.

- **Robust:**
  - Is the information/tool/app accessible across multiple platforms and with assistive technology such as screen readers?
    - Screen reader–friendly fonts
    - Access across platforms (operating systems, tablets, phones, and office software)
    - Links that make sense for navigation (provide a shortened hyperlink instead of a long URL)
    - Adaptability—students are able to adjust color, contrasts, and fonts to meet their needs

**Start here:** Check fonts to make sure that they are screen-reader friendly; presentations can be pretty and still accessible. There are multiple font-checking apps, and you can visit the WebAIM website for guidelines.

> Making lessons accessible doesn't benefit
> only students with disabilities; it benefits all students.

---

As educators, our goal is to provide an environment where all  students can access learning. While this is an altruistic goal, it is also the law. IDEA (the Individuals with Disabilities Education Act) is a U.S. federal law that provides educational services to the more than 7.5 million students with disabilities in the United States (as of 2018–19). This law provides that students ages three to twenty-one can receive educational services that are appropriate for public education, including intervention resources.

One of the purposes of this law is to ensure that all students have access to "free appropriate public education that  emphasizes special education and related services designed to meet their unique needs and prepare them for further education, employment, and independent living," and more. You can read more about the purpose and history of this law on the IDEA page of the U.S. Department of Education website (bit.ly/IDEAabout). You can also find out more about creating an inclusive classroom and lessons that are accessible for learners of all vari-abilities at CAST.org and Universal Design for Learning (UDL) (bit.ly/UDLAccessGuide). The UDL framework is based on learning sciences as to how people learn and methods for teaching in an inclusive and accessible manner.

---

## Iterate, Collaborate, Innovate

### ITERATE

"Iterate: (*verb*) to develop (a product, process, or idea) by building upon previous versions or iterations, using each version as the point of departure for refinements and tweaks." (Dictionary.com, n.d.)

Most teaching practices are iterative processes that will never be fully done.

Introducing educational technology into the classroom is no exception. As teachers add edtech to their classroom repertoire, they will keep iterating and changing how they use it, based on student learning outcomes, evolving lesson plans, and their own deepening understanding of best practices for applications.

Iteration works for student learning too. One example of edtech iteration is using a tool such as Flip to allow students to develop their responses to prompts, demonstrate their learning, or ask questions. Here's an example of how Laurel used Flip to iterate with a lesson in her classroom.

### Laurel's Experience

When I was in the classroom, I had one lesson where I asked my students to take on the roles of Founding Fathers and declare whether they were Federalist or Anti-Federalist, and whether they supported the ratification of the U.S. Constitution.

I used to have students present in person in front of the class, but once I started using Flip, I instead asked them to iterate with the help of technology. Using Flip enabled students to write a script, cite their evidence, and record their responses (with as many takes as they would like). As a teacher, I was able to iterate as well by simply changing the format in which my students presented and submitted their work. With this iteration, I was able to see, read, and hear from each of my students and evaluate their understanding and learning; this was an improvement on in-class group presentations, in which my more verbose and outgoing students would dominate the discussion, while my quiet students would stand there not speaking, making it difficult to truly evaluate their personal learning of the material. Using Flip also helped me connect with all my students because the safe and secure online environment was great for those who were shy and introverted. I could truly hear every voice in the class, and I could provide personalized feedback to each of them.

## COLLABORATE

"Collaborate: (*verb*) to work jointly on an activity, especially to produce or create something." (Lexico, n.d.)

Collaboration and technology are a powerful pairing. We see this as our students collaborate in our classrooms, but it's equally true for educators. Teachers should remember that they also don't have to go it alone; collaboration with peers and with professional learning networks is helpful, empowering, and fun. Thanks to edtech and other technological innovations, it has never been easier to bring educators together.

### A Movie Watch Party with Colleagues (Another Experience from Laurel)

When I was the incoming copresident of the ISTE Digital Citizenship Professional Learning Network (prior to the program changing to ISTE Community Leaders), my fabulous colleagues Jackie, Lauren, and I set out to create an online professional experience that would benefit our PLN members, but we faced a myriad of challenges.

Our first hurdle was finding a time when the three of us could get together to plan because we were scattered across three different time zones. Online video meetings had to be adjusted to meet the time zone constraints of our team. We also set up a shared Google Doc to keep our notes as we held a virtual discussion about how we could create a meaningful and fun professional development experience for members of our DigCit PLN.

We finally settled on hosting an online watch party of the movie *The Social Dilemma* via an online streaming service. While we streamed the movie, participants logged in and collaborated in real time in an online chat, reflecting on the movie together from all over the world. We monitored the chat and collected resources that were mentioned, later sharing those with participants on another Google Doc. As hosts, we collaborated during the event by logging into two platforms on multiple screens so we could solve any problems on a back channel.

In the end, we harnessed each of our strengths through virtual collaboration to make this idea a reality, and we had an amazing time with educators who came to the virtual party. There were a lot of (virtual) laughs in the chat, resources shared, and a great dialogue that made all our behind-the-scenes hard work and collaboration worth it. An added bonus of this experience was the community we formed: through this collaboration, I got to know my fellow ISTE DigCit PLN members (whom I had never met IRL) so much better. This experience solidified our bonds as not only ISTE colleagues but also as friends.

Virtual watch parties are a way to have a shared viewing experience of a video in real time with others. Watch parties are a great way to build community with colleagues and friends, no matter where you are located! There are a multitude of ways to host a watch party—including using a streaming service (although this usually means one or more people need to subscribe to that service), sharing a link, or logging on and pressing play at the same time. You can find out more about online watch parties and how to host and participate in one in this article from Polygon. Happy watching! bit.ly/9HostWatchParty

## INNOVATE

"Innovate: (*verb*) to make changes in something established, especially by introducing new methods, ideas, or products." (Lexico, n.d.)

To make edtech integration into the classroom more doable and less daunting, here are a few suggestions for successful implementation of a new app or online tool:

1. **Do the research.** Has this app or website been approved for use by your Instructional Technology (IT) department? Check to

see where the list of approved technology resources can be found. (Each district or LEA may house this in a different place.) If an app or website isn't approved for use, who can you talk to about getting it approved?

2. **Get support and training.** Check out training videos or watch webinars for successful implementation of the app. You don't have to reinvent the edtech wheel. Many educational technology companies provide free training and materials for teachers. The IT or educational technology department from your school or district may have resources for training as well.

3. **Set yourself and your students up for success.** Try backwards planning with a unit of study and see where the edtech tool would enhance student learning and benefit you as the teacher as well. Don't try to fit in an app or online resource just because it's the newest or "everyone" is using it.

4. **One tool at a time.** When thinking about bringing technology into the classroom, start from where you are regarding edtech integrations and then try implementing one tool at a time. Teach your students how to use the chosen application for your classroom and content and your classroom norms and expectations. Please don't assume that students know how to use an app or will know how you expect them to use it in your class with your content. Once you and your students have demonstrated proficiency with that app, then it would be appropriate to try another, and so on.

"But I'm not an innovator!" you may exclaim. "Innovators are the people who build new schools, establish nonprofits, get invited to late-night talk shows, and are prominently featured in glossy magazines." We beg to differ. The fact that you've picked up and opened this book means that you are already an innovator. Every time you try a new approach to reach a student, you're innovating. Every time you apply something new that you learned from a conference, from a colleague, from your district, you are innovating. You have all the skills you need; now let us help you apply those skills to edtech.

What does innovation look like? Here, we'll show you with a story from Karalee.

### Karalee and ThingLink

When I first started adding edtech to my classroom, I was intimidated. I started working with an instructional coach, but all of the apps overwhelmed me, and I didn't think I could learn them all. Then I decided I didn't need to learn them all; I could instead learn one thing well.

I decided to focus on ThingLink, an app that makes any image, 360° VR image, video, or 360° video into an interactive learning experience. The creator adds digital interactive tags that lead to additional engaging and informative content and media.

I signed up for the ThingLink Teacher Summer Challenge and took a deep dive into learning this one app. I completed each step of the challenge and became a skilled user. I incorporated ThingLink into my classroom, then went a step further and became a ThingLink certified trainer, and even presented on ThingLink at conferences. I created a 360° Chinese Immigrant Museum, "History Comes to Life with ThingLink 360/VR Immigrant Museum," and wrote a post on the ThingLink blog about using the app to bring part of my family history to life in this VR Immigrant Museum. My latest ThingLink 360° image, highlighting the Terminal Island Japanese Fishing Village Memorial, was recently featured in the ThingLink Celebration Collection 2021. edut.to/3OjVOYi

Once I learned this one app well, it gave me an understanding of how adding edtech to my classroom could work and the motivation and confidence to try more.

Student ThingLink Ideas:

+ annotating close reading
+ analyze primary source
+ interactive identity map
+ immigrant journey
+ immigrant oral history
+ map of journey
+ Flip reflections
+ digital portfolio
+ annotated infographic
+ video biographies for historical figures or current figures
+ annotated map

Teacher-Generated ThingLink Ideas:

+ teacher introduction
+ sharing project instructions
+ curating and sharing resources
+ 360° tour of historic sites
+ 360° classroom tour
+ digital scavenger hunt
+ choice boards
+ virtual museum to showcase student work
+ HyperDoc
+ flipped instruction: asynchronous lesson

- - - - - - - - - - - - - - - - - - - - - - - - - - - - - - - - - - - - -

## Edtech from Obstacle to Opportunity
### AN EXPERIENCE FROM KARALEE

In March 2020, across the globe, classrooms were turned upside down as teachers were abruptly thrown into pandemic teaching. And though I'm a "techy" teacher, I still struggled. Those first weeks were a crash course in remote-learning survival, and my skills were pushed to the limit; apps that before seemed fun and optional became necessary for survival. Mundane tasks taken for granted in the physical classroom, like taking attendance, seemed to take forever. I mourned the loss of our weekly community circles; building community and genuine connections with students felt like a distant memory, unattainable in the virtual classroom.

But as the weeks continued, remote learning became more comfortable. I learned to skillfully navigate Zoom, adjusted to teaching online, and found ways to connect with students and build community in authentic ways online. I was finally able to breathe and look at the possibilities and the opportunities that edtech could provide for my students.

Before the pandemic, there was one experience I had always wished I could share with my students: In 2014, I attended the Monticello Teacher Institute and spent the week immersed in Thomas Jefferson's world. I walked through his home; I followed the path those enslaved by Jefferson took to bring him the delectable meals prepared by his talented, enslaved chefs. Wandering his vast plantation deepened my understanding of our brilliant, complex, slaveholding third president. I had always wished I could bring my students with me to share in these epiphanies.

My dream came true during the pandemic. In 2020, Monticello started offering live virtual tours of Thomas Jefferson's home, and I was able to virtually travel through Jefferson's home with my students. I was impressed at how each docent emphasized that the Declaration of Independence was a blueprint, an ideal we've never lived up to, the perfect country we've never built. The docents explained that it's up to us and all future generations to strive toward this inclusive ideal. In the setting of Monticello, built and staffed by so many talented and intelligent people who were enslaved by this founding father, the contradiction of our lifelong slaveholding president writing a document declaring that all men are created equal resonated in a deep and profound way for my students, as well as for me, viewing the contradictions of Monticello through their eyes.

Check out the Monticello Teacher Institute promotional video (you might even recognize a friendly face!) and sign up to attend their summer professional development. Even if you don't attend, check out Monticello.org and classroom.Monticello.org for resources about Thomas Jefferson and the people he enslaved.

bit.ly/MTIVideo          monticello.org          classroom.monticello.org

The silver lining of pandemic teaching was learning how to leverage the possibilities that technology provided, including the ability to push out the four walls of our physical classroom and invite the world into our virtual space. Thanks to edtech, I was able to provide numerous rich and engaging experiences, as guest speakers from across the country came to speak to my kids about history, citizenship, and more. I also took my students on virtual field trips across the country to locations where history took place. These were amazing experiences that would not have been possible in person.

# Virtual Field Trips

- Detective McDevitt, Ford's Theatre: Students joined James McDevitt (portrayed by an actor), who was on duty at the Metropolitan Police Headquarters on April 14, 1865, the night President Lincoln was assassinated. Together we virtually traveled through the streets of Washington, D.C., revisiting the sites and reexamining the clues from the investigation into the Lincoln assassination conspiracy. While this experience is monetized, there are a wealth of free virtual field trips available from Ford's Theater as well (bit.ly/DetMcDevitt).

- California State Parks PORTS (Parks Online Resources for Teachers and Students): Ranger John guided students on a tour of the Angel Island Immigration Station in San Francisco, CA, a prison-like location where some 175,000 Chinese immigrants, including my grandparents, were interrogated and successfully entered the United States (ports-ca.us).

## SIMULATION

- iThrive Games: Students role-played as government officials collaboratively making decisions during "Lives in Balance," a fast-paced, engaging, realistic, and challenging online simulation about a pandemic (bit.ly/LivesBalance).

# Guest Speakers

- **Dr. Emma Humphries**, iCivics Chief Education Officer and Deputy Director of CivXNow, shared a compelling, engaging presentation on why the census matters.

- **Amy King**, fellow 2019 History Teacher of the Year, provided students with an engaging personal explanation of life in North Carolina, a swing state during a contentious presidential election.

- **Nathan McAllister**, 2010 Gilder Lehrman National History Teacher of the Year, shared his insights on his fellow Kansan and passionate abolitionist John Brown. Later in the year, Nate asked and discussed the question "Were Civil War surgeons butchers or angels?" as he captivated the students with a Civil War surgery demonstration performed on a cow leg.

- **Dr. Lindsay Chervinsky**, historian and author of *The Cabinet* shared her insights about George Washington and the beginning of the United States (bit.ly/LMChervinsky).

- **Linda R. Monk**, JD, aka The Constitution Lady, a constitutional scholar, journalist, and nationally award-winning author, shared her insights about James Madison and the creation of the Bill of Rights (bit.ly/LindaRMonk).

- **Simon Tam**, activist, author, musician, speaker, and self-proclaimed troublemaker, shared his Asian American story of being bullied, creating social change, and engaging in activism, as well as his ten-year struggle in the courts that ended with the victorious outcome in his U.S. Supreme Court case. His story, shared a week after the 2021 Atlanta shootings, resonated with my students, 70% of whom are Asian. Representation matters (simontam.org).

- Reimagine (virtual) Civics Summit was the culmination of our year of remote learning. It featured guest speakers Dr. Emma Humphries and Amber Coleman-Mortley, the Director of Social Engagement at iCivics, podcaster, blogger, and activist, who spoke to the students about citizenship.

## Edtech to Help History Come to Life

"If we teach today as we taught yesterday, we rob our children of tomorrow." (Dewey, 1916)

Here are some suggestions and resources to help with virtual exploration of history and civics for students. Again, it is important to check with your district technology department to ensure that apps or online resources have been approved for use with students.

+ **Online Simulations:** Virtual simulations for history use edtech to place students in virtual situations that can help with historical understanding. At the most basic level, they can make learning about the past fun through gamification and simulation (such as The Oregon Trail, bit.ly/OregonTrailGameFun). Done well, they can help foster historical empathy (such as Be Washington, bewashington.org). It is important to choose simulations with care. Not all simulations have content that is appropriate or culturally responsive (such as those that address slavery inadequately).

+ **Geography Edtech:** Helping students understand place and geography is essential for their understanding of history. Google Earth is a powerful tool that helps bring maps and geography to life (earth.google.com). Students can zoom in and out all around the world. Ancillary lessons and resources are also available for teachers to use. Another wonderful resource is World History Maps, which has interactive maps and timelines for students to explore (bit.ly/WorldHistoryMaps).

+ **Gamification:** Using gamification makes learning fun while often encouraging problem-solving, communication, cooperation, and with some, competition. Applications and websites such as iCivics can bring serious and complicated content to life with learning games such as *Do I Have a Right?* and *NewsFeed Defenders*. The games amplify the learning curriculum that is available through iCivics. Serious topics such as refugee rights and experiences can also be addressed through gamification. In chapter 5, Angela Lee provides a lesson plan that addresses this with the gamification from the BBC, Syrian Journey: Choose your Escape Route (bbc.in/35CbHZN). As with online simulations, vet and choose gamification experiences with care and consideration of appropriateness for your students.

+ **Timelines:** Interactive timelines bring a tried-and-true historical thinking tool (the good ol' timeline) to life for students by providing the ability to interact with the past as never before. Interactive timelines are robust supplemental tools that engage students in history. Histography has an interactive timeline replete with photos and descriptions for students to learn and engage with (Histography.io). Interactive era timelines from New American History (NewAmericanHistory. org) can be helpful for secondary students in understanding broader chronological concepts with learning resources, podcasts, and connections to Bunk (BunkHistory.org) built into the timeline. Additional learning resources for students starting in fourth grade can be found on the site as well.

+ **Online Libraries and Archives:** Both students and educators may feel overwhelmed or intimidated to use online libraries or archives, but fear not! Many online libraries have worked diligently to make their content and resources accessible and user-friendly. Some examples include the U.S. Library of Congress, which features a new selection of resources including prints, photographs, films, audio recordings, maps, manuscripts, music, digital materials, and books each month (bit.ly/USLOC). The National Digital Library of India has more than 78 million resources and is dedicated to creating a virtual repository of learning resources for students and was "designed to enable people to learn and prepare from best practices from all over the world . . ." (bit.ly/DigitalLibraryIndia).

- **Virtual Field Trips and Explorations:** There are many historic sites around the world that offer virtual field trips and interactive online activities for students, and many are free or at very low cost. Some edtech companies, such as Nearpod, have virtual field trips built into their paid platform. Many historic museums have partnered with online platforms to bring their collections to students for free, such as the Museum of the World, sponsored by the British Museum and Google Cultural Institute (bit.ly/MuseumWorld). Pear Deck has partnered with the Boston Museum of Science and more to educate and engage students (bit.ly/PearDeckCollab). CyArk is a blend of an online archive, interactive world timeline, online virtual field trips, and lesson plans, combined into one website (cyark.org). Students can engage in a variety of curated cultural and historic events and experiences with more than 200 sites on all seven continents of the world. It is worth checking out CyArk's "Journey to Equal Rights," which "amplifies the stories of activism that continue to shape our world today."

- **Podcasts:** According to an article from Cult of Pedagogy website, "just the act of listening to a good narrative helps your students become better learners. Podcasts are a screen-free, movement-enabling, ear-stimulating, and eye-opening way to deliver content. Whether you are in-person, remote, hybrid, flipped, or blended, podcasts can enhance your teaching in meaningful ways" (Patterson, 2021). We reached out to our history teachers PLN on Twitter to ask which podcasts they use with students. You can see the full curated list on our website (bit.ly/BringToLifeEdTech4).

  One consideration with podcasts that was a common item of concern from our PLN is making sure that transcripts of podcasts are available to increase accessibility for all learners. This is very important and aligns with making sure that all means all when we are thinking about educational strategies to use with our students. Some of the top picks from our PLN include *Ben Franklin's World* (bit.ly/BenFranklinWorld) for ideas and thoughts regarding historical thinking skills and sourcing and source corroboration; as well as the more U.S.-based *Civics 101* (civics101podcast.org) and *Stuff You Missed in History Class* (ihr.fm/3hSvNS0), which covers a variety of historical topics from around the world.

Karalee loves listening to *Now & Then* (bit.ly/NowAndThenPod), where historians Joanne Freeman and Heather Cox Richardson help us understand today's current events by connecting them to the past. Laurel enjoys *Presidential* (wapo.st/3MICrs) from Lillian Cunningham and the *Washington Post*, which "takes listeners on an epic historical journey through the personality and legacy of each of the American presidents."

## Edtech Wrap-Up

Whew! That was a lot! Now that you've gotten an idea of how to use edtech to connect your students to history in engaging and authentic ways, we're ready to head over to chapter 5. We're excited for you to begin applying everything you've learned as you begin to design your own lesson plan. We're also so happy to introduce you to our amazing friends—we hope that the lesson plans they share will inspire you and provide examples of strategies and tech tools you can apply to your lesson plan and in your classroom. Grab your notes! Ready? Let's go!

# #TRYONENEWTHINGCHALLENGE

| Getting Started | In the Middle | Deep Dive |
|---|---|---|
| **Self-Reflection** | | |
| How are you currently using edtech to bring history to life in your classroom? | How can you enhance an established project or lesson with edtech components? | Reflect on the POUR chart from aem.cast.org. How are you making your lessons accessible for all learners? |
| **Try One Thing!** <br><br> **A = Accessibility resources** <br><br> **ET = Edtech tools** <br><br> **V = Virtual experiences** | | |
| (A) Closed captioning <br><br> (ET) Choose one edtech tool to explore with your content <br><br> (V) Consider an online virtual experience to enhance curriculum | (A) Create/revise presentations to increase accessibility <br><br> (ET) Create a way to use your chosen edtech tool with a lesson <br><br> (V) Implement an online virtual experience | (A) Provide alt-text for images <br><br> (ET) Look for authentic ways to integrate your chosen tool into lessons/units <br><br> (V) Look for ways to combine your virtual experience with your chosen edtech tool |

Check out more "Edtech to Connect" resources on our companion website.

bit.ly/BringToLifeEdTEch4
Bring History to Life Website, Chapter 4

# CHAPTER 5

# Lesson Design & Inspiration

Congratulations—you've made it to chapter 5! (Whoo-hoo! We are genuinely applauding you; this is no small feat and an awesome accomplishment!) Now it's your turn to apply everything you've learned and begin designing your own lesson ideas and outlines. We encourage you to think of this chapter as an opportunity to think outside of the lesson plan box and reflect on how to use edtech to make history and civics come alive for your students.

To guide your lesson design, we have designed a general lesson plan template.

bit.ly/LessonTemplateBHTL
Lesson Plan Template

You can use the entire template or just pieces of it in a way that works for your personal style. In the introduction, we suggested that you collect ideas, thoughts, and notes as you progressed through the book. Now you can grab those notes and start plugging them into the template.

This template includes a sample lesson plan progression, beginning with some of the basics such as lesson topic, length of time required, and standards addressed. If you are unfamiliar with the concepts of learning intentions and success criteria, we highly recommend the work of Douglas Fisher and Nancy Frey. In short, the learning intention is what you want your students to know and be able to do at the end of a lesson. The success criteria is how you, as the educator, are going to measure student success in reaching the learning intention (Fisher & Frey, 2018). Also, as you work through the template, you will notice that there are suggestions and questions embedded to generate thoughts and considerations for your lesson design. You can use all of these questions to help with creation, or just one or two. They are meant to be used as guidance and are not required parts of the lesson.

We have provided two full lesson plans that we wrote using the provided template. Each of these lessons has morphed and changed over the years as we have grown in our capacity, not only with educational technology integrations but also as history teachers. Lesson plans are never stagnant, and we are sure that we will continue to adjust and update these lessons in the future. We will keep the most current iterations on the website, so please be sure to check there for updates and changes. You will also find a curated list of the resources that are used in our lessons on the website.

As an added bonus, we have asked several awesome members of our PLN to use this template to design lesson ideas and strategies to share with you. You can find their full lessons on our website, but here we have included a synopsis for each lesson so that you can explore and compare the varied approaches to using the template (bit.ly/BringToLifeLesson5). These contributors are passionate, award-winning, and innovative educators who are experts in their fields. The lesson ideas that they have contributed are just a tiny sampling of their expertise. You can see how they all infuse their own ideas, content areas, and edtech preferences into the template. We encourage you to look at all of the lessons (not just your grade level/content area), cherry-pick what works for you, and place these ideas into your own design template. Again, we've included our now-familiar #TryOneNewThingChallenge chart at the end of this chapter so you can reflect and plan how you will implement your lesson plan as you consider how to apply what you've learned from our book and our inspiring friends' lesson plans. We've also highlighted a "Try One Thing" for each lesson—it's never been easier to try one thing!

## LESSON DESIGN, INSPIRATION, AND IDEAS

As you explore these lesson overviews, you will see that each has a content focus and a grade-level designation. However, the strategies and structures are universal, and the learning outcomes that our contributors have shared can be applied to any content area or grade level. We hope these can help spark ideas for designing your own lessons (or iterating on what you already have!).

As you read through the lesson ideas, here are some questions that can help guide you through your exploration:

1. **What is the lesson title?**

   a. What does the title reveal about the topic/content being covered?

   b. Is this a topic I teach and can directly apply to my classroom?

   c. Do I teach a similar topic? If not, how can I adapt this lesson and/or approach to teaching a related topic?

2. **What is the grade designation?**

   a. How can I adjust the level of this lesson to match my grade level if necessary?

3. **How much time is allotted for this lesson?**

   a. Does this lesson fit into my time constraints?

   b. Do I have enough time with my curriculum to teach this entire lesson?

   c. If not, how can I adapt this lesson to fit into my class time constraints?

   d. Can I adapt and shorten this lesson if necessary?

   e. Can I extend this lesson for a deeper inquiry?

4. **What are the learning objectives (also known as learning intentions)? Do these objectives fit with my course content?**

   a. If not, can I adapt/apply similar objectives to my course content?

   b. How can I rewrite the learning objective and success criteria to meet my course and lesson objectives?

5. **What edtech tools are used in this lesson?**

   a. Have these tools been approved for use in my school/district/local education agency?

   b. If not, are there similar tools that have been approved that I can substitute in the lesson?

   c. Do I know how to use these tools?

   d. If not, where can I learn more about their use in the classroom?

e. Can I use these tools in other ways in my classroom?

6. **What is the structure used in this lesson?**

   a. How will this progression work with my students?

   b. How can I effectively iterate and apply this structure to my course content?

7. **What educational learning strategies are presented?**

   a. How can I implement these strategies in my classroom?

   b. What is a strategy that resonates with me? How can I iterate and use this strategy with my existing content?

8. **What questions do I still have?**

## Our Sample Lesson Plans

### LAUREL'S LESSON PLAN: THE U.S. INDIAN REMOVAL ACT (AN INTRODUCTION THROUGH PRIMARY SOURCES)

**Lesson Plan Overview**

This lesson is based on student historical inquiry and close reading of primary sources. The U.S. Indian Removal Act of 1830, while popular in its time, has had lasting devastating impacts on the American Indian[*] community and is generally now regarded as highly controversial legislation (at best). Students will engage in reading primary source documents and

---

[*]The term American Indian was deliberately chosen to refer to Native peoples addressed in this lesson. Guidance for correct terminology comes from the National Museum of the American Indian. (Native Knowledge 360° | Frequently Asked Questions, n.d.)

then use the knowledge they have acquired, including historical empathy and evaluating multiple perspectives, as historical evidence while engaging in a summative writing assignment. While this lesson is U.S.-specific, the concept of primary source document analysis can be applied to any controversial law from the past in the world.

**Content Area:** U.S. History

**Grade Level:** Eighth Grade

**Approximate Length:** Multi-day Lesson

This classroom lesson demonstrates use of primary sources, inquiry, and implementation of historical thinking skills. This lesson can take place over the course of multiple consecutive class periods or during two to three blocks during block scheduling. (*This is part of a larger unit entitled "Age of Jackson." For full resources and links, visit our companion website.*)

### Learning Intentions and Success Criteria

Students will examine primary source documents that relate to the U.S. Indian Removal Act that was signed into law by U.S. President Andrew Jackson in 1830. Students will further demonstrate their understanding of the ramifications of this law on American Indian communities through a summative writing assignment.

### Objectives With Grade-Level Adjustment

**Objectives:**

Students will:

+ Read, interpret, and analyze primary sources related to the U.S. Indian Removal Act
+ Demonstrate an authentic understanding of the U.S. Indian Removal Act
+ Identify the key stakeholders in the Act

+ Identify multiple perspectives regarding this legislation (popular in its day)
+ Complete a summative task at the end of the lesson addressing the EQ below.

## Essential Question (EQ):

1.  Content EQ: How did Andrew Jackson change the country (United States) through the Indian Removal Act? (CA HSS Framework p. 261)

2.  Unit EQ: Identify multiple perspectives and complexities in historical perspectives.

## Grade Level Adjustment:

+ **Younger students:** Scaffold review with primary sources (review together as a class or in small groups) and check for understanding as you review the documents. You can also have students participate in a "Think, Pair, Share" (Simon, n.d.) activity to discuss the questions with peers.
+ **Older students:** Research independently from a list of archives, sources, and databases (National Archives, Library of Congress, GALE, etc.). Discuss findings with peers in a collaborative online platform such as Padlet or shared Google Docs.

### Diversity and Inclusion Connections

This lesson focuses on a historical event; however, many connections can be made to how the U.S. Indian Removal Act has had lasting and devastating consequences for American Indians to this day.

**Further connections:** Students can research the controversies that have surrounded the renaming of sports teams and school mascots that are derogatory to American Indians.

Standards Addressed
  + ISTE Student Standards: 1.3a, 1.6a
  + Content Area Standards: CCSS ELA/HSS Grade 6-8
  + ELA-Literacy/RH/6-8/1/
  + ELA-Literacy/RH/6-8/2/

Suggested Edtech Tools for Implementation / Materials / Preparation
**Suggested Edtech Tools:**

  + Flip or online video recording tool
  + Google Slides or Microsoft PowerPoint
  + Google Docs or Microsoft Word
  + Online bulletin board such as Wakelet or Padlet
  + Chromebook/PC/tablet

**Other Materials Required:**

  + Wi-Fi/internet access

**Advance Teacher Preparation:**

  + Familiarize yourself with the website U.S. National Archives, David M. Rubenstein Collection: Records of Rights (recordsofrights.org) and primary source materials available.
  + It is highly recommended that teachers run through the entire activity ahead of time to make adjustments for any challenges they anticipate their students may come across.
  + Provide the website to students through Learning Management System or other means (Google Classroom, Canvas, Teams, Padlet, bit.ly, Wakelet, etc.).
  + Create a digital document with questions to guide students through primary sources as they relate to the EQ. *Can be printed if technological access is limited (devices or Wi-Fi).*

+ Prepare Flip topic for student responses.
+ Prepare rubric for grading based on the essential question.

Lesson Plan Steps (highlighting opportunities for more equitable access)

1. Teacher polls students for their initial thoughts on the EQ to access any prior knowledge before the webquest.

   a. Remind students of the overarching unit essential question: How did Andrew Jackson change the country (United States) through the Indian Removal Act? (CA HSS Framework p. 261)

   b. Additional questions may be included: What was the U.S. Indian Removal Act of 1830 and how did it impact American Indians, both in the past and today?"

      i. Instruct students to use their prior knowledge to answer the EQ and to make inferences based on what they have already learned in the Age of Jackson unit. (Students are not expected to be able to fully answer this question; this is the goal of the webquest investigation.)

   c. Teacher can poll students this through a variety of edtech tools (if desired), including:

      i. Mentimeter

      ii. Google/Microsoft Forms

      iii. Other tools that you like (including paper, such as sticky notes)

2. Assign students the "Understanding the Indian Removal Act" webquest (housed on companion website). This may be assigned virtually or on

paper. This webquest works most effectively with students exploring the digital resources on the website. However, if students do not have Wi-Fi access, printed paper copies of each primary source may be used for students to access, share, and study during class.

a. Teacher will give directions and model for students:

   i. How to access the website

   ii. Approximately how long this exploration should take

   iii. The amount of information students are expected to write as they explore the primary sources

   iv. How students will demonstrate their knowledge and understanding—through a rubric or peer-review?

3. Following the webquest, review the outcomes of the exploration to discuss as a whole class to dig deeper into the materials; provide clarifications and answer questions as well.

   a. Review may be conducted through small group peer review of the webquest materials and primary sources or a whole class review.

4. Students will prepare for the summative assessment.

   a. Review the summative portion of the lesson with students: the forced removal of the Cherokee from their native lands is referred to as the Trail of Tears (directions on sample).

   b. Have students prepare to "describe this march and the impact on the Cherokee and other tribes forced from their homelands."

    c. Students will take a deeper dive and study two of the documents (their choice) in depth, using the National Archives Written Document Analysis worksheet.

        i. Explain to students that this preparation will help them with the summative assignment.

5. Summative assessment: Students will respond to the EQ in a written ACE format/Exit Ticket citing textual evidence from their investigation.

    a. Provide options built in for students to communicate their knowledge and understanding for the summative assessment.

        i. Create a Flip topic for your class and/or assign the summative assessment through your LMS.

        ii. Allow students to share in small groups or pairs. If online, use breakout rooms.

6. Create a rubric while planning your unit. Teachers are recommended to share the rubric and summative assessment with students at the beginning of the lesson to provide clear expectations for students and decrease anxiety.

    a. A one-column/one-point rubric is an excellent way to streamline the expectations and focus on the learning outcomes associated with the essential question. Jennifer Gonzalez from Cult of Pedagogy has an excellent resource on her website. cultofpedagogy.com

Equity and Access Connections:
+ Immersive reader (including language translation) in Microsoft products
+ Digital and paper content available
+ Choice for summative assessment
+ Option for students to complete webquest with a partner

Civic Action Connections
+ Students research the Indigenous land their school is located on and the history of the Indigenous people local to this land. (native-land.ca).
+ Students create an Indigenous Land Acknowledgement statement using resources from the Native Governance Center (nativegov.org).
+ Students may decide to raise money as a class or school and donate to a cause that supports Indigenous people. (If there are no local charities available, consider donating to a national organization.)
+ Read Medium article: "5 Ways to Support Indigenous Communities on Indigenous People's Day"

Distance Learning/Hybrid Learning Adaptations and Considerations:
+ Students will complete webquest and document analysis asynchronously with various checkpoints assigned to check for understanding and completion. Class time will be used for assignment directions clarification, group discussion, and reflection.
+ For distance learning, all work will be assigned digitally. For students without access to Wi-Fi, the teacher will make arrangements for a paper version of materials to be sent home.

Learning Assessments (Formative/Summative)

**Formative Assessments/Feedback Loops:**
+ Check for understanding
+ Peer-to-peer review
+ Small group/whole class discussions

**Summative Assessment Options:**
  + See Step 5 in lesson plan (above)
  + Student Choice for demonstrating learning
  + Flip, Google Slides presentation, essay

Extensions for Further Learning
  + Invite American Indian speakers to class to discuss connections to the present day.
  + Research U.S. Secretary of the Interior, Deb Haaland, the first Native American to be a cabinet secretary. (Research may include what the secretary of the interior's role is in the government.)
  + Make connections to local history and local American Indian tribes/ organizations.

Try One Thing

The U.S. National Archives Written Document Analysis Worksheet is an excellent tool to help students access and assess primary and secondary source written documents. This worksheet helps students to discover the motivations of the author, the intended audience, and other document information. The scaffolded format allows students to gain a deeper understanding of written materials with a higher-level lexile/complex language to provide greater access to primary and secondary source content for students.

Bring history to life by visiting our companion website and access all the resources for Laurel's lesson plan; you can also view other lesson plans from our fabulous contributors.

 bit.ly/BringToLifeLesson5
Bring History to Life Website, Chapter 5

**KARALEE'S LESSON PLAN: MONUMENTS AND MEMORIALS**

## Lesson Plan Overview

This lesson is focused on monuments and memorials in the United States. After studying the U.S. Civil War and Reconstruction, students will engage in a primary and secondary source document investigation of the U.S. Civil War Confederate monuments and participate in a Structured Academic Controversy (SAC). This lesson culminates in a summative written demonstration of student learning. These strategies used can be adapted and applied to any monuments and memorials around the world.

**Content Area:** U.S. History

**Grade Level:** Eighth Grade

**Approximate Length:** Multi-day Lesson

This lesson demonstrates use of primary sources, inquiry, historical thinking skills, discussion and reflection, and culminates in a Structured Academic Controversy (a guided structured conversation about a controversial subject). This lesson can take place over the course of three to four class periods or during two blocks during block scheduling. (*For full resources and links, visit our companion website.*)

### Learning Intentions and Success Criteria

Students will:
+ Investigate U.S. Civil War Confederate Monuments.
+ Examine primary and secondary source documents to learn about the origins, meaning, and significance of the monuments.
+ Engage in collaborative group discussion to make informed decisions as to whether U.S. Civil War Monuments should be removed.
+ Demonstrate their understanding of the appropriateness of the monuments, individually in a Flip and collaboratively in a group exit ticket, explaining whether the monuments should be removed or not.

Objectives With Grade-Level Adjustment

**Objectives:**

Students will:

- Read, study, interpret, and analyze primary and secondary sources related to U.S. Civil War Confederate monuments.
- Explain the Lost Cause and its effect on the public memory of the U.S. Civil War.
- Participate in a Structured Academic Controversy (SAC) where they will use evidence from primary and secondary sources to answer the essential question.

**Essential Question (EQ):**

Should Confederate monuments be removed?

**Grade Level Adjustment:**

- **Younger students:** Choose a local monument or memorial that students are familiar with. Conduct a whole-class investigation. The monument exploration can be about any local monument or memorial (it does not have to be a U.S. Civil War monument). It is more important for students to consider how and whom we celebrate and memorialize—and whom we are leaving out of the narrative.
- **Older students:** Research independently from the U.S. National Parks, CyArk, and other historic sites across the world. Independently choose a monument for a deeper dive.

Diversity and Inclusion Connections

Throughout this exploration, ask students what voices are featured and what voices are missing in this monuments and memorial study.

Share monuments of lesser-known events and figures, especially featuring Black, Indigenous, and people of color (BIPOC).

## Standards Addressed

- ISTE Student Standards: 1.3a
- Content Area Standards
- Common Core Standards: CCSS WHST.6-8.7

## Suggested Edtech Tools for Implementation / Materials / Preparation

**Suggested Edtech Tools:**

- Google Slides or PowerPoint
- Digital Timeline
- Flip
- Wakelet

**Other Materials Required:**

- Wi-Fi/internet access
- Confederate Monument (Arlington National Cemetery) HyperDoc (a digital document that contains all the components of the learning cycle and the hyperlinked resources necessary for completion)
- Washington, DC, monuments ThingLink, or teacher curated collection of monuments/memorials
- "The Lost Cause: Definitions and Origins" article from the American Battlefield Trust
- "Confederate Monuments Are about Racial Conflict" video that explains the 153 years of U.S. Confederate iconography timeline
- Structured Academic Controversy instructions
- Primary source documents:
    - ProCon.org, "Historic Statue Removal - Top 3 Pros & Cons"
    - New Orleans, LA, Mayor Mitch Landrieu's address on removal of Confederate monuments video—select an excerpt appropriate for your class. You may also choose to use a transcript of his speech.
    - Whose Heritage? 153 Years of Confederate Iconography
- Structured Academic Controversy worksheet
- CyArk—cultural heritage sites

**Advance Teacher Preparation:**

- This is a powerful and engaging lesson, and it requires teacher preparation and familiarity with the resources provided.
- Teacher background material (not for students): "Teaching with Monuments and Memorials."
- There is an abundance of digital content in this lesson. Much of the content can be printed out if you do not have access to Wi-Fi. If you do have Wi-Fi, all content may be shared with students through their learning management system (LMS) or other means (Google Classroom, Canvas, Teams, Padlet, bit.ly, Wakelet, etc.).
- Curate your own collection of monuments and memorials to share with your students. (Wakelet is a great way to share digital content.)
- Review the steps for a Structured Academic Controversy.
- Provide primary source documents. There may be shared digitally through the LMS or printed out for students to study.
- Prepare Flip topics for student responses (there will be the opportunity to respond to questions with a Flip: The Essential Question and the Structured Academic Controversy Question.)
- Prepare rubric for grading based on the essential question.

Lesson Plan Steps
(highlighting opportunities for more equitable access)
Day 1

**Activity One: Engage**

1. Teacher asks students, "How do you remember special events?"

    a. Students share responses aloud or with a partner

    b. Some possible responses could include: purchase souvenirs, T-shirts, take pictures, write in a journal

2. Teacher provides a curated group of monuments and memorials for students to explore with a partner or in groups of three to four. Students will answer: What do you see (observations), think (what do you think about what you observed?), wonder (what questions do you still have?). They may write out their answer on a printed worksheet, a digital doc, a Padlet, Jamboard, or sticky notes, and share with the class.

3. Teacher defines and discusses the purpose of monuments and memorials with students. Students share monuments and memorials that they can recall from their experiences.

   a. Focus questions:

      i. What are the purposes of monuments and memorials?

      ii. Whom should we memorialize?

      iii. Is it ever appropriate to remove a monument or memorial?

4. Teacher shares/discusses some monuments and memorials (Teacher shares previously curated collection of monuments and memorials.)

5. Students discuss focus questions using the "think-pair-share" model.

## Activity Two: Monument Exploration

1. Teacher introduces the U.S. Civil War Confederate Memorial monument in Arlington National Cemetery.

   a. Remind students of focus questions.

    b.  Allow time for them to explore the monument in self-paced U.S. Civil War Confederate Memorial Monument HyperDoc.

**Day 2**

**Activity One: Review & Reflect**

1.  Students review and recall the purposes of monuments and memorials from yesterday's discussion.

2.  Students turn and talk with a partner to share their observations and discoveries from the U.S. Civil War Confederate Memorial Monument HyperDoc (available on companion website or create your own). Reflection is built into the HyperDoc, so students will be prepared to answer:

    a.  What was the purpose of this monument?

    b.  Where was it built?

    c.  Why was it built?

    d.  Do you think this is appropriate?

    e.  What did you learn?

    f.  What surprised you?

    g.  What questions do you have after studying this?

**Activity Two: Connect and Reflect**

1.  Teacher introduces and discusses the Lost Cause (a movement that describes the U.S. Confederate cause as a heroic if ultimately futile effort.

2.  Teacher shares examples of U.S. Civil War Confederate memorials.

    a.  The teacher will curate a collection of U.S. Confederate memorials on Google Slides, PowerPoint, Wakelet, or print images to hang around the classroom.

    b.  Students will study the U.S. Civil War Confederate memorials with a partner or in groups of three to four. Students will answer: What do you see, think, wonder? Teacher may provide a printed or digital worksheet for students to record their answers for each monument. Other options for recording notes: post on a Padlet, sticky notes, or Google Jamboard to share with the class.

    c.  After student investigation, the teacher leads discussion on these memorials.

        i.   What did you see, think, wonder?

        ii.  How does your understanding of the Lost Cause affect your attitude and understanding of these monuments?

        iii. Optional: groups can discuss in smaller groups, and choose a spokesperson to share with the whole class.

    d.  Teacher shares Southern Poverty Law Center graphic of "Whose Heritage? 153 Years of Confederate Iconography."

    i. "Confederate Monuments are About Racial Conflict" video—explains the timeline on the graphic. (This teacher resource/video should be viewed by teacher add ahead of time, and can be shared with class if deemed appropriate.)

    ii. In pairs, groups of three to four, or the whole class, students will study the "Whose Heritage?" timeline. This can be an informal discussion, or students may record responses with their groups. Discussion prompts for the timeline:

        01. Discuss the spikes in building U.S. Civil War Confederate monuments.

        02. Discuss the rationale of the defenders of U.S. Confederate monuments.

3. Teacher asks the students "Now what?" What should be done with U.S. Confederate monuments? Teacher shares/discusses a few possible U.S. examples:

    a. Tablet about Gabriel's Rebellion attached to Stonewall Jackson Monument, Richmond, VA (2011)

    b. Robert E. Lee Monument, Richmond, VA, vandalized (2020)

    c. Removal of Jefferson Davis Statue at UT Austin (August 2015)

    d. Confederate monument in Charleston, SC, vandalized (2015)

4. Teacher ends class with the question: What should be done with Confederate monuments?

    a. If time permits, students can share their thoughts.

  b. If time doesn't permit—ask students to respond on an exit ticket via paper or online bulletin board.

## Day 3

### Activity One: Review & Reflect

1. Teacher begins class with the essential question (EQ): What should be done with the U.S. Civil War Confederate monuments?

  a. Students will work together in table groups, reflect and discuss all of the resources they have studied and the notes they have taken.

  b. Summative assessment: Provide students choice in answering the EQ.

   i. Students will respond to the EQ in a written ACE format citing evidence from their investigation.

   ii. Students share their reflections in a (previously created) Flip reflection where they cite and explain two pieces of evidence to support their answer.

2. Students assigned pro/con article to read, annotate, take notes on, and discuss with a partner or table group after they complete their summative assessment, in order to prepare for tomorrow's Structured Academic Controversy (SAC).

**Day 4**

**Activity One: Study and Prepare**

1. This mini-unit will conclude with a Structured Academic Controversy (SAC) where students will use all the primary and secondary source documents provided to discuss what should be done with the U.S. Civil War Confederate monuments.

2. Review and annotate primary and secondary source documents to prepare for SAC.

   a. "Historic Statue Removal—Top 3 Pros & Cons"

   b. Reconstruction Timeline

   c. "Whose Heritage? 153 Years of Confederate Iconography"

   d. Article: "And That Confederate Statue is Going to Stay and It Will Look Down Upon a New Day"

3. Preparation: Share the Structured Academic Controversy worksheet with each student—may be printed or assigned digitally. Each student will record their answers for the SAC on this worksheet.

**Day 5**

**Activity One: Apply**

Structured Academic Controversy Question: Should Confederate monuments be removed?

- The whole group will be working together to answer the SAC question. It's not important what position they are assigned because the whole group will reach a consensus at the end. If students want to switch sides, they may.
- The SAC requires groups of four students. If there are extra students, there can be a group of five, or two people can partner up as a team.
- Prepare a digital or a paper exit ticket for each group to share their answer to the SAC question.

1. Students organized in groups of four

    a. Each pair assigned A or B

        i.   A = Pro: Remove Confederate Monuments

        ii.  B = Con: Keep Confederate Monuments

    b. Partners study evidence and prepare four arguments to support assigned opinion

2. Pro/Con Positions shared

    a. Team A Pro presents for two minutes (Team B Con listens, takes notes)

    b. Team B Con reflects back to Team A Pro for 1 minute

    c. Team B Con presents for two minutes (Team A Pro listens and takes notes)

    d. Team A Pro reflects back to Team B Con for 1 minute

3. **Individual Reflection:** Students will review notes, reflect on the evidence and discussion, and draw their conclusion about Confederate Monument removal.

4. **Consensus Building:** Students will discuss everything together as a group of four (review individual notes) and decide on which opinion they agree on. They will choose a spokesperson to share their position with the class, and complete the group exit ticket statement (give three to four reasons/evidence to support your opinion) provided by the teacher:

   a. We believe Confederate monuments should be removed because . . . or

   b. We believe that Confederate monuments should remain because . . .

5. Whole class discussion: Teacher calls on each group to share their conclusion.

   a. Teacher leads the whole class discussion about this process, their reflections, and findings. Did the SAC change any of their opinions? How did it feel to speak without being interrupted? Teacher may call on groups, or take volunteers.

6. Students will share their conclusions in a second Flip video and explain if they changed their original position and why or why not.

Equity and Access Connections:
+ Immersive Reader (including language translation) in Microsoft products, Wakelet
+ Digital and paper content available

- Choice for summative assessment
- Option for students to complete HyperDoc with a partner

## Civic Action Connections
Students may:

- Research local monuments and memorials in their community
- Work with their school's leadership and propose a memorial that they feel should be established at their school, possibly of an individual who significantly contributed to the school or community
- Write a proposal to the city council, requesting a monument or memorial that they feel should be installed in the community
- Create a walking tour highlighting the different monuments and memorials in the area.

## Distance Learning/Hybrid Learning Adaptations and Considerations:
- All materials can be shared/completed asynchronously.
- Slides can be presented through online presentations; online discussions can be held, with practice, in the chat.
- Jamboards, Pear Decks, shared Google Slides, and Microsoft products provide opportunities for students to interact with each other and the material.

## Learning Assessments (Formative / Summative)
**Formative Assessments/Feedback Loops:**

- Check for understanding
- Peer collaboration
- Think, Pair, Share

**Summative Assessment Options:**

- Flip videos (two topics)
- Structured Academic Controversy group exit ticket

Extensions for Further Learning
- Research other monuments of interest to students. CyArk's "Journey to Equal Rights" highlights "five places that have been pivotal in our ongoing struggle to achieve social equality."
- Students research and write a proposal to create a monument for an underrepresented figure in history.

Try One Thing

Monuments and memorials are a great way to study local, state, national, and world history.  After studying monuments and memorials, students can prepare a proposal for a monument, memorial, or public art to honor a significant historical figure, a local community hero, other exemplary present-day figure, a group of people, or a movement they feel should be honored.

Check out the latest iteration of Karalee's lesson plan with resources on our companion website and explore lesson plans created by our outstanding contributors.

 bit.ly/BringToLifeLesson5
Bring History to Life Website, Chapter 5

## Lesson Design, Inspiration, and Ideas from our PLN

We encourage you to follow these amazing educators on Twitter, where they regularly share their expertise, ideas, and suggestions (and a funny GIF or two). You can find their Twitter handles in their biographies below.

## GRADE 4: SONAL PATEL
## "I HAVE A DREAM": DR. MARTIN LUTHER KING JR.'S IMPACT ON THE U.S. CIVIL RIGHTS MOVEMENT

Twitter: @Sonal_EDU

Sonal Patel is the Digital Learning and Innovation Coordinator for her local county office of education and is a former fourth-grade teacher. She has received numerous awards and recognitions and also serves as an ISTE Community Leader.

### Content Area
This is part of a larger unit: "The U.S. Civil Rights Movement."

### Lesson Overview

**Learning Intentions:**

- Students will describe how Dr. King and his "I Have a Dream" speech contributed to the U.S. Civil Rights Movement.

- Students will construct a timeline of events that occurred around the time of Dr. King's speech.

- Students will collaborate in groups to present information collected through research on the essential question.

**Success Criteria:**

Students will demonstrate their understanding of the contributions of Dr. King's speech to the following essential questions in their collaborative presentation: How did Dr. King influence the U.S. Civil Rights Movement? How is Dr. King's speech relevant today?

- **History:** Making connections between Civil Rights past and present.

- **Civics:** Students are encouraged to consider and discuss ways that they can engage in local activities to support long-lasting change.

- **Edtech:** Edtech can be used in a variety of ways for student research and collaboration in this lesson (interactive whiteboards, slides, etc.).

- **Teaching Strategies:** Connections to prior knowledge play an important role in setting the stage for students to engage in learning via an interactive online timeline. Students participate in a collaborative group project through cycles of formative assessments and peer feedback. This lesson culminates in a summative assessment to fully capture student learning.

## Highlights

This weeklong project based learning lesson incorporates both the CCSS ELA Literacy Standards with the ISTE Standards for Students 1.3a (Knowledge Constructor) and 1.6a (Creative Communicator). This lesson provides opportunities for students to engage in research with primary source materials as well as secondary sources through interactive timelines that help bring history to life. Civic connections include opportunities for students to make connections between the past (U.S. Civil Rights Movement) and current local and national issues.

See Sonal's full lesson on our website, where you can also review the other innovative lesson plans created by our amazing contributors.

bit.ly/BringToLifeLesson5
Bring History to Life Website, Chapter 5

## Try One Thing

Interactive timelines are a great way to engage students in their learning. Students can access preconstructed timelines such as World History Maps: The World (bit.ly/WorldHistoryMaps) or can create their own through Google and Microsoft products using shared collaborative documents with their peers.

## GRADE 5: LUCRETIA ANTON
## PACIFIC NORTHWEST NATIVE AMERICANS: CONNECTIONS TO THE LAND

Twitter: @LantonHa

Lucretia Anton serves as her district's Innovation Coach TK–12, as well as a former elementary school teacher and academic coach. Lucretia regularly presents at well-known educational conferences and has previously organized educational summits for educators in her district.

### Content Area
United States History: The Land and People Before Columbus

### Lesson Overview

### Learning Intentions:

- Students will research the impact that geography, climate, and proximity to water had on Native Americans.

- Students will read multiple print and media resources

- Students will write and cite evidence from sources to support what they have learned.

- Students will engage in discussion regarding information about Pacific Northwest Native Americans and the impact the land, weather, and natural resources had on their lives.

### Success Criteria:

Students will demonstrate their understanding of new learnings about the Pacific Northwest Native Americans and their connections to the land in a collaborative setting with their peers. This collaboration utilizes edtech tools that will allow them to effectively communicate their understanding of the topic.

- **History:** Understanding the impact geography, climate, and proximity to water had on Native Americans.

- **Civics:** Students research the local history of the land their school is located on and make connections with the impact on Indigenous history.

- **Edtech:** Edtech is infused throughout this lesson plan with an emphasis on interactive slides. Alternative means for access (non-tech) are also provided.

- **Teaching Strategies:** Collaborative group research and personalized responses via video/audio format bring the Universal Design for Learning (UDL) checkpoints to life for students. The use of formative assessments through exit tickets helps drive the learning and teaching of this lesson.

## Highlights

This two-to three-day lesson incorporates both the CCSS ELA Literacy Standards with the ISTE Standards for Students 1.6 (Creative Communicator) and 1.7 (Global Collaborator). This lesson provides opportunities for students to make connections between their lives and the past through both direct instruction and peer collaboration. Civic connections include opportunities for students to research both local Indigenous people and the history of the land that their school currently resides on.

See Lucretia's full lesson on our website and check out the wide range of lesson plans designed by our award-winning contributors.

bit.ly/BringToLifeLesson5
Bring History to Life Website, Chapter 5

## Try One Thing

Digital exit tickets are a great formative assessment to monitor student learning. You can use Microsoft and Google Forms to create interactive and engaging exit tickets. Both platforms allow for data to be collected and disaggregated via online spreadsheets which enables teachers to quickly assess their students' learning levels.

## GRADE 6: STACY YUNG
## ATHENIAN DEMOCRACY

Twitter: @StacyYung

Stacy Yung is a middle school history teacher and education consultant who specializes in culturally sustaining pedagogy and integrating educational technology. She is passionate about centering student experiences and voice in the classroom and empowering students to be active citizens in their communities

### Content Area
Ancient Civilizations / World History

### Lesson Overview

### Learning Intentions:

Students will learn about the key differences between Athenian (direct) democracy and representative democracy.

### Success Criteria:

Students will be able to describe the key differences between Athenian (direct) democracy and representative democracy.

- **History:** Students apply understandings of the achievements and limitations of democratic institutions past and present.

- **Civics:** Provide examples of countries that utilize democracy as a form of government.

- **Edtech:** Edtech plays a central role in having students make connections to prior knowledge and access and acquire new learnings and understandings about democracy.

- **Teaching Strategies:** The 5E model for instruction is the basis for this lesson: Engage, Explore, Explain, Elaborate, Evaluate. This is a wonderful method to encourage students to make connections to the material.

## Highlights

This one- to two-day lesson brings to life the CCSS ELA Literacy Standards as well as the ISTE Standards for Students 1.1 (Empowered Learner) and 1.3 (Knowledge Constructor). This lesson can be broken up into smaller chunks and spread out over several days as part of a larger unit on Ancient Greece or as part of a unit on democracy. This lesson provides opportunities for students to explore concepts such as how Athenian democracy influenced democracy in the world today and for students to make connections to countries that utilize democracy as a form of government.

See Stacy's full lesson on our website and view all of the creative lesson plans designed by our amazing contributors.

 bit.ly/BringToLifeLesson5
Bring History to Life Website, Chapter 5

## Try One Thing

The 3-2-1 prompt is a great formative assessment–easy to use and provides space for student reflection after any type of content is shared (video, article, primary source doc, political cartoon, etc.). Students share:

- 3 things they learned

- 2 questions they have

- 1 connection they can make to their life today, or to something they've learned before

## GRADE 7: FRANK PISI & BARBARA LANE
## THE BLACK DEATH: CAN WE LEARN ANYTHING USEFUL FROM AN EVENT THAT HAPPENED MORE THAN 600 YEARS AGO?

Twitter:
Barbara: @barbarajlanejr      Frank: @SacActionCivics

Barbara Lane is a former secondary English teacher and has served as the English Language Arts and History-Social Science Coordinator for her local county office of education. Currently, Barbara is serving as an adjunct professor at the university level with graduate students, as well as writing and publishing with authors from across the U.S. on educational best practices.

Frank Pisi is a former history teacher and serves as the Director of History-Social Science for his county office of education. Prior to that, Frank served as part of the California Department of Education as coordinator of the Regional System of District and School Support. Frank was instrumental as the lead for the California Literacy Inquiry and Citizenship (CLIC) project as part of the California History Social Science Framework initiative.

### Content Area
This lesson is part of a larger study of the medieval era, helping students to learn about and better understand the impact of the bubonic plague on the global population.

## Lesson Overview

**Learning Intentions:**

Students will read, listen, interpret, and analyze sources related to the Black Death.

Students will understand the impact that the Black Death had on the global population during the medieval era.

**Success Criteria:**

Students will be able to explain the impact and draw conclusions from their study of the Black Death to inform potential approaches to address modern pandemics.

- **History:** Making connections between impact of and approaches to global pandemics past and present.

- **Civics:** Write a letter or create a Flip video for World Health Organization officials about how learning about past pandemics can help us address modern-day pandemics.

- **Edtech:** Students have the option to use different edtech platforms and techniques to both acquire knowledge about the Black Death as well as demonstrate their learning.

- **Teaching Strategies:** Students have the opportunity to have more agency over their learning via collaborative edtech tools and choice boards. A modified 5E model is used throughout to help drive instruction and streamline the creation of choiceboards.

## Highlights

This multi day lesson incorporates multiple learning strategies while also addressing the CCSS ELA Literacy Standards and the ISTE Standards for Students 1.3 (Knowledge Constructor) and 1.6 (Creative Communicator). While the concept of using choiceboards for student learning is not a new one, using this learning strategy in combination with educational technology options truly help bring history to life as well as make connections to current issues.

See Frank and Barbara's full lesson on our website and explore all the lesson plans designed by our distinguished contributors.

bit.ly/BringToLifeLesson5
Bring History to Life Website, Chapter 5

## Try One Thing

Virtual choiceboards are an excellent method of providing students multiple ways to access learning and demonstrate their knowledge. Consider ways that students could be provided choice in how they acquire or demonstrate their learning. (Hint: it doesn't have to be complicated. It can be "this or that," as long as a choice is provided.)

## GRADE 8: LINDSEY CHARRON
## EXPLORATION OF U.S. MANIFEST DESTINY

Twitter: @FromLindz

Lindsey Charron is a middle school history teacher and holds two master's degrees in history and educational technology. She was chosen as a James Madison Fellow in 2013 and has won numerous awards, including California Council for the Social Studies Teacher of the Year in 2020 and California State History Teacher of the Year by the Gilder Lehrman Institute of American History in 2021.

### Content Area

American Expansion—The Westward Movement

### Lesson Overview

**Learning Intentions:**

Students will demonstrate an authentic understanding of the concept of Manifest Destiny and identify different factors that motivated groups to move westward in the United States.

Students will read and interpret primary sources related to Manifest Destiny.

**Success Criteria:**

Students will analyze the consequences of U.S. expansion westward by reading primary source documents and then use the knowledge acquired to complete the summative assignment.

- **History:** Students will identify factors that motivate groups to move and the consequences of migration as they connect the past to the present.

- **Civics:** Students will research local history and examine how migration has affected the formation of their community.

- **Edtech:** Edtech provides various primary source documents for students to analyze and engage with.

- **Teaching Strategies:** Students have agency as they independently investigate the causes and consequences of U.S. Westward Expansion. They will corroborate different pieces of evidence to answer the essential questions above, providing evidence to support their claim.

## Highlights

ISTE Standard 1.3 (Knowledge Constructor) and 1.6 (Creative Communicator) as well as CCSS Literacy Standards provide the educational framework for this multi day lesson. This lesson is based on student historical inquiry, and close reading of primary sources when paired with historical empathy can lead to powerful learning opportunities for students.

See Lindsey's full lesson on our website and review all the engaging lesson plans designed by our outstanding contributors.

bit.ly/BringToLifeLesson5
Bring History to Life Website, Chapter 5

## Try One Thing

Analyzing artwork as a primary source is an excellent way to connect with the past and for students to practice their historical analysis skills. The British Museum of the World in Google Cultural Institute is a highly engaging resource that marries interactive timelines with art to make meaningful connections for students. britishmuseum.withgoogle.com

## GRADE 9: ANGELA LEE
## STUDENT RESPONSE AND ACTION IN THE AGE OF GLOBAL MIGRATION

Twitter: @MrsHistoryLee

Angela Lee is a world history educator who serves on the Massachusetts Department of Education's History and Social Studies Standards Review panel, as well as the World History Association (WHA) Teaching Committee. She previously served on the advisory board for the National Endowment for the Humanities (NEH) funded project, World History Commons. She is a leader in the Advanced Placement World History community throughout the United States.

### Content Area
World History–Migration

### Lesson Overview

**Learning Intentions:**

Students will define terms: "migrant," "refugee," "asylum seeker," and "internally displaced persons (IDP)".

Students will engage in a simulated digital journey of Syrian refugees and learn about refugees' stories.

**Success Criteria:**

- **History:** Students connect the historic consequences of forced migration to the current refugee crisis.

- **Civics:** Students engage in a design challenge to brainstorm possible action plans and write a proposal to carry out an action plan to help refugees.

- **Edtech:** Edtech is infused throughout this highly engaging lesson. Students explore various online resources to empathetically understand the refugee experience.

- **Teaching Strategies:** Student dialogue and collaborative strategies, as well as the use of online simulations and current examples, help build and foster empathy—both historically and contemporary.

## Highlights

This multi day lesson is part of a year long focus on migration in a ninth-grade world history course. It can be modified for modern world history, world geography, world cultures, or contemporary issues courses. Students will explore the difference between voluntary and involuntary migration through student discussions, online simulations, and examination of primary sources. Both the CCSS Literacy Standards and ISTE Standards 1.1 (Empowered Learner) and 1.3 (Knowledge Constructor) form the pedagogical basis and framework of this engaging lesson.

See Angela's full lesson on our website and website and check out the wide ranging lesson plans designed by our outstanding contributors.

bit.ly/BringToLifeLesson5
Bring History to Life Website, Chapter 5

## Try One Thing

There are many different online "Choose Your Own Adventure" (CYOA) or interactive simulation experiences for students to explore. It is a great way to bring historical empathy into the lesson and topic. Students can create their own CYOA through interactive slides or forms on both the Microsoft and Google platforms.

## GRADE 10: WHITNEY OLSON & ANNE OLSON
## ANALYZING THE PAST TO CHART THE FUTURE:
## INTRO TO HISTORIOGRAPHY

Twitter: Whitney: @WhitneyOlson62          Anne: @EquityAnnie

Whitney Olson is the co-coordinator for National History Day in California through the Sacramento County Office of Education. She works with teachers across California to bring historical research, historical thinking skills, and analysis to their curriculum and students. Whitney is a former secondary teacher and is currently finishing her master's degree in history through the Gilder Lehrman Institute of American History.

Anne Olson currently teaches secondary education and specializes in Advanced Placement U.S. History, U.S. History, and Gender Studies. She is passionate about bringing her students authentic learning experiences that reflect the work of academic historians as opposed to the rote memorization that most history curriculum requires.

### Content Area
Historiography Unit

### Lesson Overview

### Learning Intentions:

Applying the principles of historiography, students will engage in civic and historical dialogue on an undecided historical dilemma.

Student-driven discourse and application of historical literacy and inquiry will challenge students to find their voice and connect social issues to their historical roots.

**Success Criteria:**

Students will engage in civic and historical deliberation on an undecided historical dilemma connecting social issues to their historical roots by examining the essential questions: Where does the history of the United States ultimately begin? How? When? And perhaps, above all, why do historians now approach the early American historical landscape differently?

- **History:** Learning the process of historiography and historical thinking skills fosters connections to social issues for students.

- **Civics:** This lesson provides foundational civic background for students by making connections to their historical roots in order to take informed civic action.

- **Edtech:** Edtech options provide equity of student voice and feedback.

- **Teaching Strategies:** The use of primary sources, direct quotes, and peer interactions helps students create an understanding of the significance of historical events.

## Highlights

This lesson includes opportunities for students to engage in deep discussion on the way history is written, potential conflicting objectives and narratives, and how our understanding of history is shaped by cultural and other factors. Students are guided through the use of primary sources and direct quotes to examine and dive deeper into the dual role of a historian, as well as how historians influence the present with their work and enlighten the present when they provide interpretations of the past. Utilizing the CCSS Literacy Standards and ISTE Standards 1.2 (Digital Citizen) and 1.3 (Knowledge Constructor) brings the opportunities for students to build their skills in crafting evidentiary claims and going beyond the surface with the analysis.

See Whitney and Anne's full lesson on our website and survey all the lesson plans designed by our innovative contributors.

bit.ly/BringToLifeLesson5
Bring History to Life Website, Chapter 5

**Try One Thing:**

Consider sharing direct quotes as part of your lessons. Ask students to reflect and share what the quote means to them and how it connects to the lesson. Both primary and secondary source quotes are valuable for students to examine and engage in historical empathy and historiography.

## GRADE 11: NATHAN MCALLISTER
## MUSEUM STUDIES: ARTIFACT INVESTIGATION

Twitter: @NHTOYmc

Nathan McAllister is currently serving as the Humanities Program Manager–History, Government, and Social Studies with the Kansas State Department of Education and was a former secondary history teacher for more than twenty years. He was named the Kansas and National History Teacher of the Year by the Gilder Lehrman Institute for American History in 2010. Nate serves on the boards of several state and national organizations, including the Kansas Council for History Education and the iCivics National Educators Network, and is the head of the Lowell Milken Center for Unsung Heroes Curriculum Committee.

### Content Area
Museum Studies

### Lesson Overview

### Learning Intentions:

Students will learn how to analyze primary source artifacts and infer the different usages of historical artifacts.

Students will draw conclusions and make inferences based on non-linguistic features.

### Success Criteria:

Students will demonstrate their understanding of primary source artifacts by summarizing their understanding of the impact of historical artifacts on their understanding based on the following essential questions: How are artifacts from the past similar and different to artifacts of the present? What do artifacts from the past tell us about the people who used them? What can we infer about the impact of the artifact?

- **History:** Compare and contrast artifacts from the past and present. Reflect on what they tell us about the people who used them.

- **Civics:** Research local history and identify a significant artifact that affected your community's development.

- **Edtech:** Edtech provides  access to a variety of online images of historical artifacts for students to investigate. Students will share their takeaways with online tools.

- **Teaching Strategies:**  In pairs or groups,  students will collaborate, observe, analyze, and dialogue as they investigate a primary source artifact.

## Highlights

This multiday inquiry-based lesson is built around primary source artifacts and an opportunity for students to take the lead through authentic investigation and analysis of artifacts. The CCSS Literacy Standards and ISTE Standards 1.5 (Computational Thinker) and 1.6 (Creative Communicator) support the learning that students engage in through historical inquiry.

See Nate's full lesson on our website and review all the amazing lesson plans designed by our remarkable contributors.

bit.ly/BringToLifeLesson5
Bring History to Life Website, Chapter 5

## Try One Thing:

An artifact is an engaging way to teach our students how to study and learn about the past. Select an artifact to share, then guide your students through the inquiry process. Ideas include:

- School memorabilia

- An object from the teacher's past

- A modern-day object

## GRADE 12: AMY KING
## GO LOCAL! THE POWER OF TEACHING HISTORY THROUGH A LOCAL LENS

Twitter: @KingHistoryCCHS

Amy King is a secondary history teacher as well as an adjunct professor in higher education. Amy has received many awards and recognitions for her contributions to education, including being named as a 2021 Grosvenor Teacher Fellow with National Geographic and Lindblad Expeditions, the 2019 Gilder Lehrman North Carolina History Teacher of the Year & National Finalist, and receiving the 2019 NCSU College of Education EdTalks Outstanding Alumni Award.

### Content Area

Place-based local history—taking macro (historical events, ex.: the U.S. Civil War) and analyzing the impact on the local community (micro).

### Lesson Overview

### Learning Intentions:

Students will engage in inquiry through local historical place-based history.

Students will engage in discussion surrounding the impact on the local community based on historical events.

### Success Criteria:

Students will engage in project based learning and provide detailed analysis based on their historical research through collaborative student work.

- **History:** Students learn to analyze the impact historical events have on local communities.

- **Civics:** Students may publish their findings about local history in order to inform their community of the impact of historical events.

- **Edtech:** Digital archives provide access to local history primary resources. Students will collaborate and share research in a digital curation tool, and share their takeaways digitally.

- **Teaching Strategies:** Teacher guides, supports, and provides students choices as they conduct their own local historical investigation.

## Highlights

Steeped in historical inquiry, this multi day lesson is intended to provide students with the opportunity to engage in learning how larger historical events (macro-level, such as World War II) had an impact on their local community (micro-level). Given the opportunity to consider essential questions to drive the research and inquiry process, students can make deeper connections and foster historical empathy in their local community. CCSS Literacy Standards as well as ISTE Standards 1.3 (Knowledge Constructor) and 1.7 (Global Collaborator) provide the framework for student learning.

See Amy's full lesson on our website and review all the outstanding lesson plans designed by our celebrated contributors.

bit.ly/BringToLifeLesson5
Bring History to Life Website, Chapter 5

## Try One Thing

Bring one local connection from your community into your classroom that is connected to a larger event in history to help students make connections between micro and macro history. Ideas for possible connections include:

- Guest speakers (community member, city council member, school board member, etc.)

- Newspaper articles

- Historic locations

- Local monuments

- Local museums or archives

# Chapter Wrap-Up

## #TRYONENEWTHINGCHALLENGE

| Getting Started | In the Middle | Deep Dive |
|---|---|---|
| **Self-Reflection** | | |
| What lessons are you already teaching that could benefit from one of the strategies highlighted in the lesson samples and snapshots? | What are ways that you can take an existing lesson and reimagine it based on what you have read in this book? | What lesson would you create or reimagine using multiple edtech tools, lessons, or strategies that were outlined in chapters 1 through 4 and sample lessons and ideas? |
| **#TryOneNewThingChallenge!** | | |
| Choose one strategy or tech tool from the sample lessons to implement in your classroom. | Incorporate ideas generated from the lessons, strategies, and tech tools from chapters 1 through 4 and the sample lesson plans as you design your own lesson to make history come to life. | Plan and implement your newly designed edtech lesson plan to bring history to life in your classroom. |

Get more ideas and lesson plan inspiration by viewing all the lesson plans on our companion website.

bit.ly/BringToLifeLesson5
Bring History to Life Website, Chapter 5

# CONCLUSION

## Beginnings . . .
### AN EXPERIENCE FROM KARALEE AND LAUREL

**February 28, 2020**

**Karalee:**

The hotel reception room was filled with history educators devouring hors d'oeuvres and anxiously waiting for the program to begin. It was Friday night at the annual conference of the California Council for the Social Studies (CCSS). I was there to celebrate my dear friend Lindsey, the recipient of the CCSS Outstanding Middle School Teacher of the Year. I'd always found these receptions awkward and uncomfortable, so standing next to a tiny table in the dimly lit room with no chairs, making small talk with history educators while precariously balancing a hot bite-sized appetizer on my napkin, was not my idea of the perfect Friday night. I was relieved when Stacy appeared, another dear history teacher friend and fellow Lindsey fan. After cheering for Lindsey and our other amazing colleagues, we hung around to chitchat and take the requisite pictures and selfies.

"I know you, History Frog!" A sophisticated and impressive-looking woman with a beautiful head of red hair bounded across the crowd, coming straight at me. If she hadn't uttered my Twitter handle, @HistoryFrog, I

© *Laurel Aguilar-Kirchhoff*

would have been certain she was greeting someone else. Why, out of the countless people in this room, was she addressing me? I recognized her signature red hair, as I had been following her on Twitter; she had impressed me, while at the same time my imposter syndrome made me feel out of her league. Her Twitter profile picture was amazing: it showed her seated on a yellow modern accent chair, with a confident but friendly smile, her voluminous red hair gently resting on her left shoulder, beautifully contrasting her dark teal blazer. Her tweets interacted with professional organizations and discussed National History Day, women's leadership, and other important topics that were even more impressive. I just tweeted the "frog tastic" happenings in my classroom; my Twitter picture was my Bitmoji, and I wasn't really active in any professional organizations. Could two people be any more different?

**Laurel:**

Same ballroom, same hors d'oeuvres, different point of view. When I saw the group of fantastic women educators across the ballroom at the CCSS Awards ceremony, I was nervous: I recognized them all from our PLN and various sharing of resources, thoughts, and best practices through Twitter, but I had never met any of them IRL. I had to gather my courage to go over and introduce myself and see if we could talk without a screen between us (and more than the 280 characters allowed in a tweet).

I saw the bob haircut of my Twitter friend, @HistoryFrog. I knew her name was Karalee, but I had no idea if she would recognize me and if this IRL introduction would be welcome when she was obviously surrounded by friends and colleagues whom she *did* know IRL. Would there be an awkward silence and staring at our feet and around the room after the initial rush of saying "Hi, hello, how are you?"

I shoved the last of my carrot stick crudité into my mouth, buckled up my courage, and forced myself to cut a path across the room right toward my online friends. I just came out and said, "Hi! I know you. You're @HistoryFrog! I'm @LucyKirchh. Well, Laurel, really. I don't know if you recognize me, but we know each other on Twitter! I can't believe we are here in real life!" (Yes, I speak in exclamation points!)

Of course, my fears about the introductions were for naught: Karalee, Lindsey, and Stacy were just as kind, wonderful, and welcoming in person as they were from behind the screen. We chatted, laughed, congratulated Lindsey, and took selfies—after all, we had met our history-social science PLN buddies IRL, and Twitter expected to see the evidence! I was excited to meet them, and they made me feel welcome. I couldn't wait to see where we could go as a PLN and as a friend group now that we had finally met.

**Karalee & Lucy:**

Little did we realize how much life would soon change in our world, in our country, in ourselves, and in our new friendship that had been birthed in that brief exchange. The following month, the world shut down due to the COVID-19 pandemic. As we, along with the rest of the world, learned to navigate during a pandemic, we began to do life together: working from home, introspecting and reflecting as women, remote learning moms, educators, citizens, dear friends, and—eventually—as coauthors of this book.

• • • • • • • • • • • • • • • • • • • • • • • • • • • • • • • • • • • • • • •

## If We Can Do It . . . You Can Too!

All teachers' educational journeys are unique and intensely personal. We haven't been "perfect" teachers; there are plenty of stories of epic classroom fails that we haven't included in this book. There were plenty of times when we could have thrown up our hands in frustration, but we are both committed lifelong learners who continue to fail forward, get up, learn from our experiences (and each other), and iterate. We have adopted the philosophy of the wonderfully wise Maya Angelou (to paraphrase): Know Better, Do Better.

Let us reassure you—often the road is not clear, and just when we think we have it all figured out, life will sometimes remind us that we don't. With that said, if we can do this, we know you can, too!

**Laurel:** I went from a science and history middle school teacher who loved PBL to Teacher of the Year for National History Day California. That didn't happen because of luck, but because of a willingness to learn, grow, and sometimes utterly fail. I was fortunate to connect with a real-life PLN on my campus that supported my edtech adventures as well as helped me host History Day workshops in the computer lab. Being able to reach out and connect with other educators from across the world opened my professional and educational eyes and heart, which in turn led me to try out new educational practices, work toward becoming certified in as many edtech apps as I possibly could, and be willing to try new things. This led to my becoming a Google Certified Trainer, as well as serving as an ISTE Community Leader. Now, I have opportunities to help others through my work and the communities that I am grateful to be a part of. I am proud of my journey with the triumphs and tragedies that have occurred along the way (shout out to my fave National History Day theme!). If I can do it, you can too!

**Karalee:** I went from being a long time U.S. history middle school teacher who loved technology and history, to California History Teacher of the Year and being featured in *Time* magazine. I started collaborating with my fellow history teachers from day one, before collaboration was a word commonly used. Instructional coaches helped me to incorporate edtech into my classroom in authentic and meaningful ways, providing space, safety, and support for me to reflect and refine my practices, as well as to be able to fail, iterate, and try again. Interaction and collaboration with amazing educators in my district, across the nation, and in the Twitterverse has brought the world into my classroom, deepened my historical and civics understandings, helped me grow professionally and personally, and provided me with numerous opportunities to interact, collaborate, grow, share, encourage, and support others in their educational journeys. I am grateful for my journey, with all the challenges and the triumphs. If I can do it, you can too!

## Call to Action
Now that you have read our book, let's continue our growth through building a community dedicated to sound historical inquiry practices with

an infusion of civics, which uses the power of edtech to bring history to life. We invite you to the #TryOneNewThingChallenge! Go back through our book, check out a tool or strategy you'd like to try, revisit a topic that resonated with you, or reflect on the Try One New Thing table at the end of each chapter and commit to trying one new thing. Share your new thing with our community on Twitter or the social media platform of your choice using the hashtag #TryOneNewThingChallenge, and don't forget to tag us in the post. Let's build a community that iterates, collaborates, and innovates to bring history to life for all of our students!

Speaking of communities, there are some wonderful communities that you can join through the ISTE Connect discussion boards. Thousands of ISTE members from around the world ask questions and offer advice on a host of topics. You can connect on virtually any subject, discover more resources, and attend (or watch archived) ISTE Expert Webinars by authorities in their fields. (Laurel presented the ISTE Expert Webinar on Digital Citizenship in October of 2021!) Joining an ISTE community is easy: log in to your ISTE account and go to the ISTE Commons page. You can search by topic or browse through the latest discussion posts. It is a great way to get involved and join an educator community.

We appreciate the time that you have taken to read this book. We hope it has brought you insights, challenged you, and provided resources for you and your students. Though you have reached the end of the book, you have not reached the end of your history journey, or our time together. We invite you to explore our book's companion website, where you will find countless resources to support you as you continue to bring history and civics to life for your students.

And since we have spent so much time together—it's been like a history happy hour; we've even shared a beverage or two!—we consider you a friend and invite you to become a part of our PLN and Twitter community. We love hanging out with our friends, and we would love hanging out (virtually) with you. Come follow us—@LucyKirchh, @HistoryFrog, and our book @BringHistoryToLife—on Twitter, use the hashtag #BringHistoryToLife, and join our amazing online community of fellow educators who are dedicated to making a difference in the minds, hearts, and lives of their students. We're a community of people who love talking about history, civics, empathy, and edtech (if you haven't figured this out by now), and we'd love to continue this conversation and hear about the amazing things you are doing in your classroom. If we can do it, you can too!

Happy History!
Laurel & Karalee

 bit.ly/KaraleeTwitter

 bit.ly/LucyKirchhTwitter

 bit.ly/BringHistoryToLifeTwitter

Being a part of the ISTE Community has a lot of educational perks, including access to professional development webinars created and presented by experts from around the world. Check out Laurel's ISTE Expert Webinar, "The BIG 3: DigCit, MediaLit and SEL Connections in the Digital Age of Learning." You can download the webinar using the link, or you can find the archive of past ISTE Expert Webinars by logging into ISTE Connect. Learn, be inspired, and get involved in the ISTE community! bit.ly/LaurelExpertWebinar

# REFERENCES

African Academic Network on Internet Policy. (n.d.). *AANIoP blog.* https://aanoip.org/category/blog/

Aguilar-Kirchhoff, L. (n.d.-a). *Indian Removal Act—multiple perspectives.* https://drive.google.com/file/d/1I r06kpbA4XAyBFnwLsYQ78peIHaAZlzc/view?usp=sharing

Aguilar-Kirchhoff, L. (n.d.-b). Sample lesson plan template. https://docs.google.com/document/d/1Tl77G PndcfJDJc0Q4XIANbVI50d6h4JT_C_-8Ts0_As/copy

Aguilar-Kirchhoff, L. (2019). Understanding the Indian Removal Act. https://drive.google.com/ file/d/1_ckhD6wArUDNeNHB9f8amCIAe9GFHi1C/view

Aguilar-Kirchhoff, L. (2021, September 21). Licks, Toilets & TikTok . . . *MotivatED Learning.* https://www. lucykirchh.com/post/licks-toilets-tiktok

Aguilar-Kirchhoff, L. (2021, October 19). The BIG 3: DigCit, MediaLit and SEL connections in the digital age of learning. *ISTE Connect.* https://connect.iste.org/community/calendar/event-description?Cal endarEventKey=8aef4bf1-a1b3-43ea-ab91-9dab5e15d8af&CommunityKey=da1c31e1-349a-4f40- b51e-8471c433babb&Home=%2Fhome

Aguilera, J., Carlisle, M., & Reilly, K. (2021, September 2). From teachers to custodians, meet the educators who saved a pandemic school year. *Time.* https://time.com/6094017/ educators-covid-19-school-year/#karalee-wong-nakatsuka

Ahmed, A. (2021, July 27). Explained: How the student data breach leaves minors vulnerable to several threats. *Firstpost: Tech2.* https://www.firstpost.com/tech/news-analysis/explained-how-the-student- data-breach-leaves-minors-vulnerable-to-several-threats-9839511.html

American Battlefield Trust. (2021, July 14). The lost cause: Definition and origins. https://www.battlefields. org/learn/articles/lost-cause-definition-and-origins

American Library Assocation. (n.d.). *American Association of School Librarians.* https://www.ala.org/aasl/

Annenberg Public Policy Center. (n.d.). Institutions of democracy. https://www. annenbergpublicpolicycenter.org/political-communication/

BBC News. (2015, April 1). Syrian journey: Choose your own escape route. https://www.bbc.com/news/ world-middle-east-32057601

Belaud, V. (2018, April 3). Teachers and students' data protection and privacy in the upcoming EU General Data Protection Regulation. European Trade Union Committee for Education. https://www.csee- etuce.org/en/news/2529-teachers-and-students-data-protection-and-privacy-in-the-upcoming-eu- general-data-protection-regulation

British Museum, The. (n.d.). *The museum of the world.* https://britishmuseum.withgoogle.com/

Burke, L. & Baker McNeill, J. (2011, January 5). "Educate to innovate": How the Obama plan for STEM education falls short. Heritage Foundation. https://www.heritage.org/education/report/educate-innovate-how-the-obama-plan-stem-education-falls-short

CAST. (2021, October 15). *The UDL guidelines*. https://udlguidelines.cast.org/

Common Sense Education. (2021, October 25). Challenging confirmation bias. https://www.commonsense.org/education/digital-citizenship/lesson/challenging-confirmation-bias

Chervinsky, L. (2021, January 11). Why you should participate in an (online) book club. *Harvard University Press Blog*. https://harvardpress.typepad.com/hup_publicity/2021/01/why-you-should-participate-in-an-online-book-club.html

Cinelli, M., De Francisci Morales, G., Galeazzi, A., Quattrociocchi, W., & Starnini, M. (2021, February 23). The echo chamber effect on social media. *PNAS*. https://doi.org/10.1073/pnas.2023301118

Coleman-Mortley, A. (Host). (2021, December 8). Historical empathy, making it real for kids with Dr. Katie Perrotta [Audio podcast episode]. *Let's K12 Better*. https://letsk12better.buzzsprout.com/1036873/9688670-historical-empathy-making-it-real-for-kids-with-dr-katie-perrotta

Columbia Center for Teaching and Learning. (n.d.). Community building in the classroom. https://ctl.columbia.edu/resources-and-technology/teaching-with-technology/teaching-online/community-building/

Common Core Stand Standards Initiative. (n.d.). English language arts standards. http://www.corestandards.org/ELA-Literacy/

Cox-Richardson, H., & Freeman, J. (Hosts). (n.d.). *Now & then*. https://podcasts.voxmedia.com/show/now-then

Covart, L. (Host). (n.d.). *Ben Franklin's world*. https://benfranklinsworld.com/

Crittenden, J., & Levine, P. (2018, August 31). Civic education. *Stanford Encyclopedia of Philosophy*. https://plato.stanford.edu/entries/civic-education/

Cunningham, L. (Host). (n.d.). *Presidential: A podcast about the character and legacy of America's presidents*. https://www.washingtonpost.com/graphics/business/podcasts/presidential/

Davenport, M. (2016, September 22). Socratic seminars: Building a culture of student-led discussion. *Edutopia*. https://www.edutopia.org/blog/socratic-seminars-culture-student-led-discussion-mary-davenport

Debroy, A. (2019, May 2). How can institutions prepare students to become global citizens? *EdTechReview*. https://edtechreview.in/trends-insights/insights/3497-prepare-students-to-become-global-citizens

Dewey, J. (1916). *Democracy and education*. New York: Macmillan.

Dictionary.com. (n.d.). | *Meanings and Definitions of Words at*. Retrieved April 18, 2022, from https://www.dictionary.com/

Duckworth, S. (2020, March 2). *#SketchnoteFever*. https://sylviaduckworth.com/sketchnotefever/

Dutch, J. [Julie] (2014, August 10). *Philosophical chairs* [Video]. https://youtu.be/19elwVxjfeA

Ebert, W. (2018, May 8). Help your students A.C.E. response to text writing. *TeachWriting.Org.* https://www.teachwriting.org/blog/2018/4/30/qtczd76hbqpoy2x0rs7qg9j2fcf28c

Education Staff, National Archives and Records Administration. (n.d.). Written document analysis worksheet. U.S. National Archives. https://www.archives.gov/files/education/lessons/worksheets/written_document_analysis_worksheet_former.pdf

Endacott, J., & Brooks, S. (2013). An updated theoretical and practical model for promoting historical empathy. *Social Studies Research and Practice, 8*(1), 41–58. https://doi.org/10.1108/ssrp-01-2013-b0003

Facing History and Ourselves. (n.d.). What is Community? [Lesson]. https://www.facinghistory.org/resource-library/identity-and-community/what-community

Farah, K., & Arnett, T. (2019, July 25). How edtech can expand what teachers do. *Edutopia.* https://www.edutopia.org/article/how-edtech-can-expand-what-teachers-do

Federal Trade Commission. (2020, December 1). *Children's Online Privacy Protection Rule ("COPPA").* https://www.ftc.gov/legal-library/browse/rules/childrens-online-privacy-protection-rule-coppa

Finley, T. (2014, August 12). Establishing classroom norms. *Edutopia.* https://www.edutopia.org/blog/establishing-classroom-norms-todd-finley

Fisher, D., & Frey, N. (2021, June 16). Show & tell: A video column / A map for meaningful learning. https://www.ascd.org/el/articles/a-map-for-meaningful-learning

Flip. (n.d.). Let's be GridPals. https://info.flip.com/blog/tips/gridpals.html

Ford's Theatre. (n.d.). Set in stone [Teacher program]. https://www.fords.org/for-teachers/programs/set-in-stone/

Freeman, J. [Host]. (n.d.). *History Matters (. . .and so does coffee!).* National Council for History Education. https://ncheteach.org/conversation-post/History-Matters-and-so-does-coffeeI

Freeman, J. (2020, August 17). Being a historian during historic times. *The Atlantic.* https://www.theatlantic.com/ideas/archive/2020/08/historian-historic-times/615208/

Fuller, K. (2021, December 16). 5 ways to support Indigenous communities on Indigenous Peoples' Day (and every other day). *Medium.* https://medium.com/illumination/5-ways-to-support-indigenous-communities-on-indigenous-peoples-day-and-every-other-day-df5c4ca9120e

Garrison, D. R, Anderson, T., & Archer, W. (2000). CoI Framework. Community of Inquiry. https://coi.athabascau.ca/coi-model/

George Washington's Mount Vernon. (n.d.-a). *Be Washington interactive experience.* https://www.bewashington.org/

George Washington's Mount Vernon. (n.d.-b). *Situation room experience: Washington's cabinet.* https://www.mountvernon.org/education/situation-room-experience-washingtons-cabinet/

Global Read Aloud. (2021, July 23). About the GRA. https://theglobalreadaloud.com/for-participants/

Goldsmith, S. (1993). *A city year: On the streets and in the neighborhoods with twelve young community service volunteers*. The New Press.

Gonzalez, J. (2021, August 19). Meet the single point rubric. *Cult of Pedagogy*. https://www.cultofpedagogy.com/single-point-rubric/

Haje, L. (2020, September 9). Projeto visa proteger dados pessoais de estudantes nas plataformas de ensino a distância. *Câmara dos Deputados* [Brazil]. https://www.camara.leg.br/noticias/695042-projeto-visa-proteger-dados-pessoais-de-estudantes-nas-plataformas-de-ensino-a-distancia/

Hall, A. (2017, July 18). Reflecting the past, reflecting the present. *Colloquy* (Summer 2017). Harvard University Graduate School of Arts and Sciences. https://gsas.harvard.edu/news/stories/reflecting-past-reflecting-present

Hellesen, R. (n.d.). Investigation: Detective McDevitt. *Ford's Theatre*. https://www.fords.org/visit/virtual-events-and-special-tours/history-on-foot/

iCivics. (n.d.). Who we are. https://www.icivics.org/who-we-are

International Society for Technology in Education. (2022). ISTE Standards for Educators. https://iste.org/standards/iste-standards-for-teachers

International Society for Technology in Education. (2022). ISTE Standards for Students. https://iste.org/standards/iste-standards-for-students

iThrive Games Foundation. (2020, March 4). *iThrive Sim*. https://ithrivegames.org/ithrive-sim/

Jones, C. (2019, April 18). Alexander's biggest talent was pushing the other Founding Fathers' buttons, says the Yale expert advising 'Hamilton: The Exhibition.' *Chicago Tribune*. https://www.chicagotribune.com/entertainment/theater/ct-ae-hamilton-exhibition-history-0421-story.html

Kaufman, T. (2022, March 3). Building positive relationships with students: What brain science says. *Understood*. https://www.understood.org/articles/en/brain-science-says-4-reasons-to-build-positive-relationships-with-students

Leaver, E. (2021, October 26). How to run a school penny war fundraiser. *PTO Today*. https://www.ptotoday.com/pto-today-articles/article/8400-how-to-run-a-school-penny-war-fundraiser

Lee, E. (2021). *America for Americans: A history of xenophobia in the United States*. Basic Books.

Levin, K. (2018, May 9). "And that Confederate statue is going to stay and it will look down upon a new day." *Kevin M. Levin*. http://cwmemory.com/2018/05/09/and-that-confederate-statue-is-going-to-stay-and-it-will-look-down-upon-a-new-day/

Levine, P. (2014). Civic renewal. *Peter Levine: A Blog for Civic Renewal*. https://peterlevine.ws/?page_id=11

Lexico. (n.d.). *Collaborate* [Definition]. Oxford University Press. https://www.lexico.com/en/definition/collaborate

Lexico. (n.d.). *Innovate* [Definition]. Oxford University Press. https://www.lexico.com/en/definition/innovate

Luther King, Jr., M. (1963, August 23). *Martin Luther King, Jr.* [Exhibit]. National Archives at New York City. https://www.archives.gov/nyc/exhibit/mlk

Mai, L. (2018, May 27). Use historical empathy to help students process the world today. *Facing Today*. https://facingtoday.facinghistory.org/use-historical-empathy-to-help-students-process-the-world-today

McCarthy, H. & Capodice, N. (Hosts). (n.d.). *Civics 101 podcast*. https://www.civics101podcast.org

Miller, T. (2019, August 29). Mayor Pro Tem Roger Chandler's comments infuriate Arcadia residents. *Arcadia Weekly*. https://issuu.com/beaconmedianews/docs/2019_08_29_regional_pubs__arc

Monticello Teacher Institute. [TeachMonticello]. (2015, February 4). *Monticello teacher institute 2014* [Video]. https://youtu.be/Y_yDnB7Y4DY

Moore, T. (2011, May 20). *How to tie your shoes* [Video]. TED Conferences. https://www.ted.com/talks/terry_moore_how_to_tie_your_shoes

Museum of the Moving Image. (n.d.). For teachers. *The living room candidate*. http://www.livingroomcandidate.org/lessons

Nakatsuka, K. (2017, October 27). History comes to life with Thinglink 360/VR immigrant museum. *Thinglink Blog*. http://thinglinkblog.com/2017/10/27/history-comes-to-life-with-thinglink-360vr-immigrant-museum/

National Center on Accessible Educational Materials. Access to learning. https://aem.cast.org/get-started/access-learning

National Center on Accessible Educational Materials. (2021, April 21). Designing for accessibility with POUR. https://aem.cast.org/create/designing-accessibility-pour

National Council for the Social Studies. (2013). College, career, and civic life (C3) framework for social studies state standards. https://www.socialstudies.org/standards/c3

National Constitution Center. (n.d.). We the civics kids. https://constitutioncenter.org/learn/educational-resources/we-the-civics-kids

Native Governance Center. (2022, February 15). *A guide to Indigenous land acknowledgment*. https://nativegov.org/news/a-guide-to-indigenous-land-acknowledgment/

Native Knowledge 360° | Frequently Asked Questions. (n.d.). Teaching & Learning about Native Americans: Terminology. https://americanindian.si.edu/nk360/faq/did-you-know

New Zealand History. (2021, July 27). Historical empathy. Research and Publishing Group of the New Zealand Ministry for Culture and Heritage. htztps://nzhistory.govt.nz/te-akomanga/historical-concepts/empathy-historical

PBS Learning Media, Bess, M. (Host). (2021, February 24). Why do our brains love fake news? Above the Noise [Video]. *Above the Noise*. PBS LearningMedia. https://ca.pbslearningmedia.org/resource/bias-brain-kqed/why-do-our-brains-love-fake-news-above-the-noise/

Perrotta, K. (2018, October 13). Welcome to Dr. Perrotta's "The Elizabeth Jennings project!" https://elizabethjenningsproject.wordpress.com/

Plaisance, P. (2019, May 9). Virtue in the media world. *Psychology Today*. https://www.psychologytoday.com/us/blog/virtue-in-the-media-world/201905/the-dilemma-empathy-and-the-news

ProCon.org. (2022, January 27). Historic statue removal—Top 3 pros & cons. *Britannica*. https://www.procon.org/headlines/historic-statue-removal-top-3-pros-cons/

Pew Research Center (2021, May 28). Public trust in government: 1958–2021. https://www.pewresearch.org/politics/2021/05/17/public-trust-in-government-1958-2021/

Radulovic, P. (2021, December 23). 9 ways to watch movies with friends on Netflix, Disney, Hulu and more. https://www.polygon.com/21295526/how-to-watch-movies-with-friends-together-online-netflix-party-hulu-kast-disney-plus-watch2gether

Read Write Think. (n.d.). Using the think-pair-share technique [Strategy guide]. National Council of Teachers of English. https://www.readwritethink.org/professional-development/strategy-guides/using-think-pair-share

Ripp., P. (2019, September 23). Mystery Skype: Where in the world are they? International Society for Technology in Education. https://www.iste.org/explore/In-the-classroom/Mystery-Skype%3A-Where-in-the-world-are-they%3F

Robinson, J. (1965, May 9). Jackie Robinson, civil rights advocate. U.S. National Archives. https://www.archives.gov/education/lessons/jackie-robinson/telegram-1965.html

Ronald Reagan Presidential Foundation & Institute. (n.d.). *Air Force One discovery center*. https://www.reaganfoundation.org/education/discovery-center/

Roosevelt, T. (1904, May 27). *Letter from Theodore Roosevelt to William W. Justice*.

Theodore Roosevelt Center. https://www.theodorerooseveltcenter.org/Research/Digital-Library/Record?libID=o188263

Simon, C. A. (n.d.). Using the Think-Pair-Share Technique | Read Write Think. Read Write Think. https://www.readwritethink.org/professional-development/strategy-guides/using-think-pair-share

Southern Poverty Law Center. (n.d.). Whose heritage? 153 years of Confederate iconography [Infographic]. https://www.splcenter.org/sites/default/files/com_whose_heritage_timeline_print.pdf

Shapiro, S. & Brown, C. (2018, February 21). The state of civics education. Center for American Progress. https://www.americanprogress.org/article/state-civics-education/

Stanford Encyclopedia of Philosophy. (2018). Civic education. Stanford University. https://plato.stanford.edu/entries/civic-education/

Steinmetz, K. (2013, July 3). 'Impudent huzzy!': How to speak like a founding father. *Time*. https://newsfeed.time.com/2013/07/03/impudent-huzzy-how-to-speak-like-a-founding-father/

Swartzer, K. (2019, May 28). 10 reasons to use sentence frames in your classroom. *The Chalk Blog*. https://www.learnersedge.com/blog/10-reasons-to-use-sentence-frames-in-your-classroom

Swann, S. (2021, October 6). Massive investment in civic education proposed to reinvigorate democracy. *The Fulcrum*. https://thefulcrum.us/civic-ed/civic-education-investment

Teachinghistory.org. (n.d.a). Structured academic controversy (SAC). https://teachinghistory.org/teaching-materials/teaching-guides/21731

Teachinghistory.org. (n.d.b). Teaching with monuments and memorials. https://teachinghistory.org/best-practices/using-primary-sources/24079

Thinglink Collection (n.d.). Celebration collection 2021 welcome & introduction. https://www.thinglink.com/scene/1529795620913545217

Thomas Jefferson Foundation. (n.d.). *Monticello teacher institute*. https://www.monticello.org/research-education/for-educators/monticello-teacher-institute/

United Nations. (1948, December 10). *Universal declaration of human rights*. https://www.un.org/en/about-us/universal-declaration-of-human-rights

United Nations. (2020). *Global Education Monitoring Report 2020: Inclusion and Education - All Means All*. United Nations.

U.S. Department of Education. (n.d.). *Family Educational Rights and Privacy Act (FERPA)*. https://www2.ed.gov/policy/gen/guid/fpco/ferpa/index.html

U.S. Department of Education. (2001). *No Child Left Behind Elementary and Secondary Education Act (ESEA)*. https://www2.ed.gov/nclb/landing.jhtml

U.S. Department of Education. (2021, February 28). *Individuals with Disabilities Education Act (IDEA)*. https://sites.ed.gov/idea/

U.S. National Archives. (n.d.). *Situation Room Experience*. https://situationroom.archives.gov/

Vasilogambros, M. (2021, May 19). After Capitol riot, some states turn to civics education. *Stateline*. https://www.pewtrusts.org/en/research-and-analysis/blogs/stateline/2021/05/19/after-capitol-riot-some-states-turn-to-civics-education

Visit Oregon. (2022, February 2). *The Oregon trail game online*. https://www.visitoregon.com/the-oregon-trail-game-online/

Vox. (2017, August 23). *This timeline shows confederate monuments are about racial conflict* [Video]. https://youtu.be/WClgR6Q0aPE

Walther, M. (2018, June 26). Ancient history belongs in schools. *The Week*. https://theweek.com/articles/781034/ancient-history-belongs-schools

Wilson, T. & Frey, H. (Hosts). (n.d.). *Stuff You Missed in History Class* [Podcast]. iHeartRadio. https://www.iheart.com/podcast/stuff-you-missed-in-history-cl-21124503/

Whitby, T. (2013, November 18). How do I get a PLN? *Edutopia*. https://www.edutopia.org/blog/how-do-i-get-a-pln-tom-whitby

Williams, J. (2019). *Teach boldly: Using edtech for social good* (Illustrated ed.). International Society for Technology in Education.

Wineburg, S., & McGrew, S. (October 6, 2017). Lateral reading: Reading less and learning more when evaluating digital information ISTE. *Stanford History Education Group Working Paper No. 2017-A1.* https://doi.org/10.2139/ssrn.3048994

Winthrop, R. (2020, June 4). The need for civic education in 21st-century schools. *Brookings.* https://www.brookings.edu/policy2020/bigideas/the-need-for-civic-education-in-21st-century-schools/

World History Maps. (2021, April 3). *World history maps – Welcome to atlas of world history.* https://www.worldhistorymaps.info/

Zúñiga, C. G., Cárdenas, P., Martínez, R., & Valledor, L. (2019). Teachers' classroom practices for citizenship education: Experiences of teachers rated as outstanding. *Citizenship, Social and Economics Education, 19*(1), 3–22. https://doi.org/10.1177/2047173419887972

# INDEX

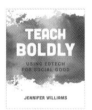